GOVERNMENT PROCEDURES AND OPERATIONS

EMERGENCY LENDING BY THE FEDERAL RESERVE

BACKGROUND AND POLICY ISSUES

Government Procedures and Operations

Additional books in this series can be found on Nova's website under the Series tab.

Additional e-books in this series can be found on Nova's website under the eBooks tab.

GOVERNMENT PROCEDURES AND OPERATIONS

EMERGENCY LENDING BY THE FEDERAL RESERVE

BACKGROUND AND POLICY ISSUES

FELICIA ESTRADA
EDITOR

nova publishers
New York

Library of Congress Cataloging-in-Publication Data

ISBN: 978-1-63485-393-4

Published by Nova Science Publishers, Inc. † New York

CONTENTS

PREFACE

The deepening of the financial crisis in 2008 led the Federal Reserve (Fed) to revive an obscure provision found in Section 13(3) of the Federal Reserve Act (12 U.S.C. 344) to extend credit to nonbank financial firms for the first time since the 1930s. Section 13(3) provides the Fed with greater flexibility than its normal lending authority. Using this authority, the Fed created six broadly based facilities (of which only five were used) to provide liquidity to "primary dealers" (certain large investment firms) and to revive demand for commercial paper and asset-backed securities. More controversially, the Fed provided special, tailored assistance exclusively to four firms that the Fed considered "too big to fail"—AIG, Bear Stearns, Citigroup, and Bank of America. This book provides a review of the history of Section 13(3), including its use in 2008. It discusses the Fed's authority under Section 13(3) before and after the Dodd-Frank Act. It then discusses policy issues and legislation to amend Section 13(3), including H.R. 3189, which passed the House on November 19, 2015.

In: Emergency Lending ...
Editor: Felicia Estrada

ISBN: 978-1-63485-393-4

Chapter 1

FEDERAL RESERVE: EMERGENCY LENDING*

Marc Labonte

SUMMARY

The deepening of the financial crisis in 2008 led the Federal Reserve (Fed) to revive an obscure provision found in Section 13(3) of the Federal Reserve Act (12 U.S.C. 344) to extend credit to nonbank financial firms for the first time since the 1930s. Section 13(3) provides the Fed with greater flexibility than its normal lending authority. Using this authority, the Fed created six broadly based facilities (of which only five were used) to provide liquidity to "primary dealers" (certain large investment firms) and to revive demand for commercial paper and asset-backed securities. More controversially, the Fed provided special, tailored assistance exclusively to four firms that the Fed considered "too big to fail"—AIG, Bear Stearns, Citigroup, and Bank of America.

Credit outstanding (extended in the form of cash or securities) authorized by Section 13(3) peaked at $710 billion in November 2008. At present, all credit extended under Section 13(3) has been repaid with interest and all Section 13(3) facilities have expired. Contrary to popular belief, the Fed earned profits of more than $30 billion and did not suffer any losses on transactions authorized by Section 13(3). These transactions exposed the taxpayer to greater risks than traditional lending to banks

---

* This is an edited, reformatted and augmented version of a Congressional Research Service publication R44185, prepared for Members and Committees of Congress, dated January 6, 2016.

through the discount window, however, because in some cases the terms of the programs had fewer safeguards.

The Fed's use of Section 13(3) in the crisis raised fundamental policy issues: Should the Fed be lender of last resort to banks only, or to all parts of the financial system? Should the Fed lend to firms that it does not supervise? How much discretion does the Fed need to be able respond to unpredictable financial crises? How can Congress ensure that taxpayers are not exposed to losses? Do the benefits of emergency lending outweigh the costs, including moral hazard? How can Congress ensure that Section 13(3) is not used to "bail out" failing firms? Should the Fed tell Congress and the public to whom it has lent?

The restrictions in Section 13(3) placed few limits on the Fed's actions in 2008. However, in 2010, the Dodd-Frank Wall Street Reform and Consumer Protection Act (P.L. 111-203) added more restrictions to Section 13(3), attempting to ban future assistance to failing firms while maintaining the Fed's ability to create broadly based facilities. On December 18, 2015, the Fed promulgated a final rule implementing these changes. The Dodd-Frank Act also required records for actions taken under Section 13(3) to be publicly released with a lag and required the Government Accountability Office (GAO) to audit those programs for operational integrity, accounting, financial reporting, internal controls, effectiveness of collateral policies, favoritism, and use of third-party contractors. Although Section 13(3) must be used "for the purpose of providing liquidity to the financial system," some Members of Congress have expressed interest in—while others have expressed opposition to—the Fed using Section 13(3) to assist financially struggling entities, including states, municipalities, and territories of the United States.

House Financial Services Committee Chairman Jeb Hensarling contends that "Dodd-Frank tried but failed to rein in the Fed's emergency lending authority." In the 114th Congress, legislation— including H.R. 2625, H.R. 3189, and S. 1320—has been introduced that would limit the Fed's discretion under Section 13(3). On November 19, 2015, H.R. 3189 was passed by the House. Section 11 of H.R. 3189 would require the approval of three-quarters of the Fed regional presidents to activate Section 13(3), tighten the definition of solvency, limit borrowers to financial firms, and provide a formula for setting the interest rate above market rates. Federal Reserve Chair Janet Yellen contends that this bill would "essentially repeal the Federal Reserve's remaining ability to act in a crisis." A Fed governor has opposed further reducing the Fed's discretion under Section 13(3) on the grounds that the Fed needs "to be able to respond flexibly and nimbly" to threats to financial stability.

INTRODUCTION

The financial crisis that began in 2007 and deepened in 2008 was the worst since the Great Depression. The federal policy response was swift, large, creative, and controversial, creating unprecedented tools to grapple with financial instability. Particularly notable were the actions taken by the Federal Reserve (Fed) under its broad emergency lending authority, Section 13(3) of the Federal Reserve Act (12 U.S.C. 344). This obscure section of the act was described in a 2002 review as follows: "To some this lending legacy is likely a harmless anachronism, to others it's still a useful insurance policy, and to others it's a ticking time bomb of political chicanery."[1]

Under normal authority, the Fed faces statutory limitations on whom it may lend to, what it may accept as collateral, and for how long it may lend. Because many of the actions it took during the crisis did not meet these limitations, Section 13(3) was used to authorize most of the Fed's emergency facilities created during the crisis to provide credit to nonbank financial firms. More controversially, the Fed also invoked Section 13(3) to prevent the failure of Bear Stearns and American International Group (AIG), two financial firms that it deemed "too big to fail." The Federal Reserve (Fed) also lent extensively to banks through the discount window and newly created facilities and undertook "quantitative easing" (large scale purchases of Treasury and mortgage-backed securities) during the crisis.[2] Because these actions were taken under its normal authority, they are beyond the scope of this report, as are other actions taken by the federal government during the crisis.[3]

The Dodd-Frank Wall Street Reform and Consumer Protection Act (hereinafter, the Dodd-Frank Act; P.L. 111-203) limited the Fed's discretion under Section 13(3), but some Members of Congress believe that these changes were insufficient. This report provides a review of the history of Section 13(3), including its use in 2008. It discusses the Fed's authority under Section 13(3) before and after the Dodd-Frank Act. It then discusses policy issues and legislation to amend Section 13(3), including H.R. 3189, which passed the House on November 19, 2015.

HISTORY OF SECTION 13(3)

One of the main reasons the Fed was created was to act as a "lender of last resort," by providing liquidity in the form of short-term loans to banks through the discount window. The Fed still provides that service today, but the amount of liquidity extended is insignificant typically. Over time, it became expected that banks would meet their short-term borrowing needs through private markets under normal conditions. Discount window lending to banks occurs under the Fed's normal statutory authority.

Nonbank financial firms also face liquidity needs, but the history of Fed lending to nonbanks is much more limited. Section 13(3) has been invoked rarely since it was enacted in 1932. The Fed used it to make 123 loans to nonfinancial firms totaling $1.5 million from 1932 to 1936, until that authority was superseded by new authority (Section 13b, which was subsequently repealed).[4]

Section 13(3) can also be used to authorize lending to banks. After 1936, the Fed invoked Section 13(3) occasionally to make nonmember banks and credit unions eligible to borrow at the discount window before 1980, when nonmember banks were permitted to access the discount window.[5] Section 13(3) authority was not used to extend credit to nonbanks from 1936 to 2008. This authority was then used extensively beginning in 2008 in response to the financial crisis—in very different ways than it had been used previously.

Use of Section 13(3) in 2008

Section 13(3) was used to authorize multiple actions taken by the Fed when financial conditions worsened at two points in 2008—around the time the investment bank Bear Stearns experienced difficulties in March and following the failure of the investment bank Lehman Brothers in September. Credit extended under Section 13(3) in 2008 can be divided into two broad categories:

1. broadly based facilities to address liquidity problems in specific markets and
2. exclusive, tailored assistance to prevent the disorderly failure of individual firms deemed too big to fail.[6]

Credit outstanding (in the form of cash or securities) under Section 13(3) peaked at $710 billion in November 2008.[7] Currently, all credit extended under Section 13(3) has been repaid with interest and all 13(3) facilities have expired.[8] Contrary to popular belief, the Fed did not suffer any losses on transactions taken under Section 13(3) and earned profits of more than $30 billion (more than half of which is AIG[9] related).[10] Nevertheless, some of these transactions exposed the taxpayer to greater ex ante risks than the discount window because the terms of the programs had fewer safeguards—in some cases involving non-recourse loans[11] and troubled asset purchases, for example. The next two sections summarize this experience, with more detail provided in the *Appendix.*[12]

Broadly Based Facilities

The Fed created six broadly based facilities under Section 13(3) in 2008 to extend credit to all eligible borrowers within a particular class of nonbank financial firms or to a particular segment of financial markets:

- The *Term Securities Lending Facility (TSLF) and the Primary Dealer Credit Facility (PDCF)* were created to assist primary dealers (a group of investment firms that are the Fed's counterparties for open market operations). The Fed made short-term loans through the PDCF and TSLF to primary dealers to ensure that other primary dealers did not experience liquidity crises in the wake of the primary dealer Bear Stearns's financial difficulties.
- The *Asset-Backed Commercial Paper Money Market Mutual Fund Liquidity Facility (AMLF), the Commercial Paper Funding Facility (CPFF),* and the *Money Market Investor Funding Facility (MMIFF)* were created to support the commercial paper market (the MMIFF was never used). Commercial paper is short-term debt issued by financial firms (including banks), nonfinancial firms, and pass-through entities that issue asset-backed securities (ABS). The Fed set up its commercial paper facilities after a run on money market mutual funds forced the latter to contract their large holdings of commercial paper.
- The *Term Asset-Backed Securities Loan Facility (TALF)* was created to support the ABS market. Through TALF, the Fed made three- and five-year loans to private investors to encourage them to purchase ABS other than residential mortgage-backed securities (MBS).[13] ABS are an alternative way that banks and nonbanks finance loans to consumers and businesses, and they are often referred to as a form of *shadow banking*—activities that substitute for traditional bank lending and deposit-taking.[14] The decline in the value and liquidity of ABS

during the crisis resulted in a sharp contraction in their issuance, reducing the credit available to households and businesses.

Table 1 provides a summary of the terms and uses of these facilities. All the facilities except for TALF were used to provide short-term liquidity—conceptually comparable to the role of the discount window. The CPFF was the largest facility, and TALF was the smallest. As can be seen in the table, none of these facilities extended credit after 2010.

Figure 1 plots loans outstanding for these five facilities from March 2008, when the first facility was created, to October 2014, when the last loan was repaid. Usage of the facilities spiked beginning in mid-September 2008, peaked in December 2008, and then tapered off relatively quickly in 2009 as financial conditions stabilized. From 2010 to 2014, there were only residual amounts of credit outstanding through TALF. According to GAO, use of the facilities was relatively concentrated among a small number of borrowers—which may reflect concentration in those markets.[15]

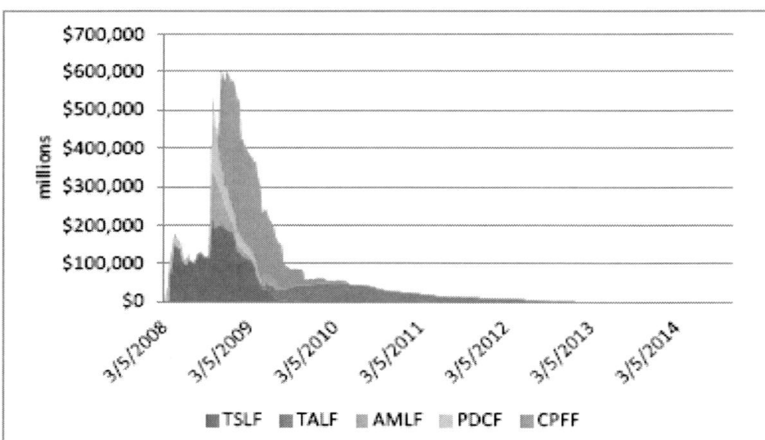

Source: Federal Reserve, H.4.1 release, various dates.

Notes: For TSLF, lending took the form of Treasury securities. For CPFF, commercial paper was purchased. For other facilities, lending took the form of cash. See Appendix for details.

Figure 1. Loans Outstanding Under Broadly Based Facilities. (March 2008-October 2014)

Table 1. Broadly Based Facilities Created in 2008 Under Section 13(3)

Usage				Terms and Conditions			
Facility	Loans Outstanding at Peak	Total Income	Number of Participants	Lending Rate/Fee	Recourse/Haircut	Term	DateAnnounced-Expired
Term Securities Lending Facility (TSLF)	$235.5billionon Oct. 1, 2008	$0.8 billion	18	Set at auction, with minimum fee of 10 to 25 basis points	Yes/Yes	28 days	Mar. 11, 2008-Feb.1, 2010
Primary Dealer Credit Facility (PDCF)	$146.6billionon Oct. 1, 2008	$0.6billion	18	Rate set equal to Fed's discount rate; fees of up to 40 basis points for frequent users	Yes/Yes	overnight	Mar. 16, 2008-Feb.1, 2010
Asset-Backed Commercial Paper Money Market Mutual Fund Liquidity Facility (AMLF)	$152.1 billionon Oct. 1, 2008	$0.5 billion	11 from 7 bank holding companies	Fed's discount rate	No/No	120 or 270 days	Sept. 19, 2008-Feb.1, 2010
Commercial Paper Funding Facility (CPFF)	$348.2billion on Jan.21, 2009	$6.1 billion	120	Markups of 100 to 300 basis points over overnight index swap rate; fees of 10 to 100 basis points	No/No	90 days	Oct. 7, 2008-Feb.1, 2010

Table 1. (Continued)

Usage			Terms and Conditions				
Facility	Loans Outstanding at Peak	Total Income	Number of Participants	Lending Rate/Fee	Recourse/Haircut	Term	DateAnnounced-Expired
Term Asset-Backed Securities Loan Facility (TALF)	$48.2 billionon Mar.17, 2010	$1.6 billion to Fed; $0.7billion to Treasury	177	Various markups over LIBOR or federal funds rate; 10 to 20 basis point administrative fee	No/Yes	5 years for CMBS, 3 years for other	Nov. 25, 2008-Mar. 31, 2010 (June 30, 2010,for new CMBS)

Sources: Federal Reserve, Office of the Inspector General, The Federal Reserve's Section 13(3) Lending Facilities to Support Overall Market Liquidity, November 2010; Federal Reserve, Quarterly Report on Federal Reserve Balance Sheet Developments, various dates. U.S. Government Accountability Office, Federal Reserve System: Opportunities Exist to Strengthen Policies and Processes for Managing Emergency Assistance, GAO-11-696, July 21, 2011.

Notes: Expiration date for facilities marks date after which no new activities were authorized. For some facilities, existing loans remained outstanding after the expiration date. Some facilities did not begin operations on the date announced. Recourse only includes to participant's assets; the Fed had recourse for AMLF and TALF only in the case of material misrepresentation.

Special Assistance to Firms Deemed "Too Big to Fail"

Section 13(3) was also invoked to provide exclusive, tailored assistance to prevent the disorderly failure of four large financial firms on an ad hoc basis:

- In March 2008, the Fed assisted JP Morgan Chase's takeover of Bear Stearns to prevent the latter's failure. Assistance was provided through first, a short-term bridge loan and then, the purchase of Bear Stearns troubled assets, financed through a $29 billion Fed loan;
- In September 2008, the Fed prevented AIG's failure by initially providing it a line of credit of $85 billion. The assistance was restructured several times, with the loan eventually replaced by a Fed pledge to purchase up to $52.5 billion in troubled assets in November (and the rest of the assistance shifted to Treasury);
- In November 2008, the Fed, Treasury, and the Federal Deposit Insurance Cooperation (FDIC) announced a joint agreement to guarantee a more than $300 billion portfolio of Citigroup's troubled assets;
- In January 2009, the Fed, Treasury, and FDIC announced a joint agreement to guarantee a $118 billion portfolio of Bank of America's troubled assets to assist its takeover of Merrill Lynch. (The agreement was never finalized.)

These actions were motivated by concerns that the failure of any of these firms would increase financial instability—in other words, the Fed viewed the firms as too big to fail or too interconnected to fail.[16] In all four cases, the Fed did not limit its action to those of a traditional lender of last resort because problems at the firms were not limited to a need for short-term liquidity. In the Fed's view, the firms were not insolvent, but were vulnerable to losing access to funding markets which could cause their failure.[17] An evaluation of whether these four institutions were solvent at the time was hampered by the "fog of war"—the Fed was forced to judge their solvency hastily in the context of a crisis, in which the value of all assets was rapidly declining and it was uncertain whether the decline was temporary or permanent. While some have described this assistance as a bail out of failing firms, in all four cases, there was not clear evidence that the firms were insolvent in the classic sense.[18] In the case of Bear Stearns, JP Morgan Chase was willing to pay more to acquire it than the value of the Fed's assistance, but later reported losses related to the transaction.[19] The other three firms all eventually returned to profitability once the crisis had ended, which means they may or may not have been solvent at the time of the intervention.

As notable as whom the Fed assisted is whom it chose not to assist—Lehman Brothers. Although Lehman Brothers was an investment firm similar to Bear Stearns, the Fed chose not to help facilitate its takeover by Barclays. Instead, Lehman Brothers filed for bankruptcy. Then-Chairman Bernanke later testified that the Fed declined to assist Lehman Brothers because it held inadequate collateral[20]—although some of the Fed's other interventions under Section 13(3) featured concerns about inadequate collateral. While one cannot say what would have happened in the counterexample where the Fed had assisted Lehman Brothers, Lehman Brothers' failure marked the worsening of the financial crisis.

Troubled assets were purchased from Bear Stearns and AIG through three limited liability corporations (LLCs) created and controlled by the Fed named Maiden Lane. *Figure 2* shows loans outstanding to the Maiden Lanes and directly to AIG. The direct loan to AIG was paid off in 2011. The asset holdings and loans of the Maiden Lanes tapered off slowly until 2011, when the pace accelerated. The final Maiden Lane loan was fully repaid in 2012; final profits to the Fed will not be known until residual asset holdings are extinguished. Although Citigroup and Bank of America were banks, this assistance was nevertheless authorized under Section 13(3) because it took the form of asset guarantees. The guarantees to Citigroup and Bank of America are not shown in *Figure 2* because Fed funds were never extended under those guarantees.

LIMITS ON EMERGENCY LENDING

Under normal authority, the Fed faces statutory limitations on whom it may lend to, what it may accept as collateral, and for how long it may lend.[21] If the Fed wishes to extend credit that does not meet these criteria, it can initiate assistance under Section 13(3).

Restrictions on Emergency Lending in Place in 2008

Section 13(3) was not in the original Federal Reserve Act of 1913; it was added in 1932 (47 Stat 715). Until the Dodd-Frank Act of 2010, the authority was very broad, with few limitations. It required that[22]

- at least five of the seven Fed governors find that there are "unusual and exigent circumstances"[23]—while this phrase has no specific legal definition, it implies that financial conditions are not normal;[24]
- the Fed may "discount (for) any individual, partnership, or corporation"—that is, assistance should take the form of a loan, and the loan may be made to private individuals or businesses;
- the borrower must present "notes, drafts, and bills of exchange endorsed or otherwise secured to the satisfaction of the Federal Reserve Bank"—that is, the loan must be backed by collateral approved by the Fed;[25]
- the Fed shall charge an interest rate consistent with the same limitations applied to the discount window;[26] and
- "the Federal Reserve Bank shall obtain evidence that such individual, partnership, or corporation is unable to secure adequate credit accommodations from other banking institutions"—that is, there must be evidence that the borrower does not have private alternatives.

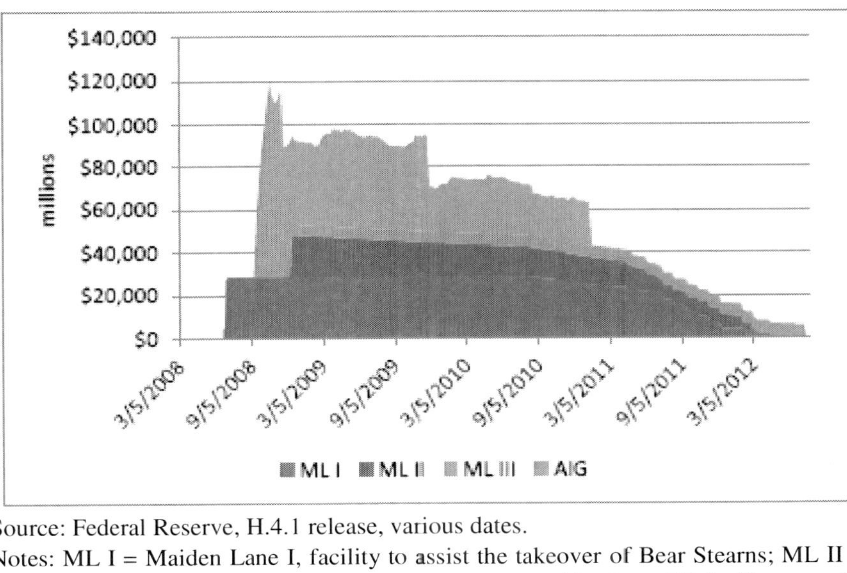

Source: Federal Reserve, H.4.1 release, various dates.

Notes: ML I = Maiden Lane I, facility to assist the takeover of Bear Stearns; ML II = Maiden Lane II, facility to assist AIG: ML III = Maiden Lane III, facility to assist AIG; AIG = direct loan from Fed to AIG. Funds were never extended under asset guarantee to Citigroup and Bank of America.

Figure 2. Loans Outstanding for Special Assistance.

These restrictions did not prevent the Fed from taking several unorthodox actions in 2008. Notably, in some cases, "In form, these transactions were structured as loans. But in substance, they permitted the Fed to move assets off the balance sheets of these institutions and onto its own."[27] In the cases of AIG and Bear Stearns, the Fed purchased their assets through limited liability corporations that it created and controlled (called Maiden Lane I, II, and III). This structure allowed the Fed to comply with Section 13(3) because the asset purchases were financed through loans from the Fed to the Maiden Lanes. The loans were backed by those assets and were eventually repaid when the assets were sold off or matured.[28] In the cases of Citigroup and Bank of America, the firms were offered a guarantee in the event that they suffered losses on a portfolio of assets, structured as a loan "provided ... on a nonrecourse basis, except with respect to interest payments and fees."[29] The Fed also made a loan directly to AIG backed by the company's general assets, meaning there were no specific securities pledged in the event of nonpayment.[30] Furthermore, the Fed has interpreted "unusual and exigent circumstances" to mean that assistance should be temporary, but routinely extended each facility's expiration date until demand for credit had waned.

One statutory revision to Section 13(3) affected the Fed's actions in 2008. In 1991, the Federal Deposit Insurance Corporation Improvement Act (P.L. 102-242; 12 U.S.C. 1811) contained a provision that removed the requirement that collateral be "of the kind and maturities made eligible for discount for member banks" at the discount window. According to the sponsor, Senator Christopher Dodd, the rationale for the provision was to enable the Fed "to make fully secured loans to securities firms in instances similar to the 1987 stock market crash."[31] Securities firms, it was argued, would not necessarily hold the same sort of assets that banks used as collateral at the discount window. By removing this language, the Fed had discretion to lend against a broader array of assets.

Changes in the Dodd-Frank Act

Concerns in Congress about some of the Fed's actions under Section 13(3) during the financial crisis led to the section's amendment in Section 1101 of the Dodd-Frank Act. Generally, the intention of the provision in the Dodd-Frank Act was to prevent the Fed from bailing out failing firms while preserving enough of its discretion that it could still create broadly based facilities to address unpredictable market-access problems during a crisis.[32] Specifically, the Dodd-Frank Act

- replaced "individual, partnership, or corporation" with "participant in any program or facility with broad-based eligibility";
- required that assistance be "for the purpose of providing liquidity to the financial system, and not to aid a failing financial company." It ruled out lending to an insolvent firm, defined as in any bankruptcy, resolution, or insolvency proceeding;
- required that loans be secured "sufficient(ly) to protect taxpayers from losses," and that collateral be assigned a "lendable value" that is "consistent with sound risk management practices";
- forbade "a program or facility that is structured to remove assets from the balance sheet of a single and specific company";
- required any program "to be terminated in a timely and orderly fashion"; and
- required the "prior approval of the Secretary of the Treasury."[33]

Proponents of the Dodd-Frank Act believed that the Fed's authority to provide assistance to too big to fail firms was no longer necessary because of other changes in the act. The Fed justified its special assistance to too big to fail firms during the crisis on the grounds that these firms could not be wound down without causing financial instability under existing law because of perceived shortcomings of the bankruptcy process. Fed officials called for the creation of a resolution regime for non-banks modeled on the FDIC's bank resolution regime so that such assistance would not be necessary in the future.[34] Title II of the Dodd-Frank Act created such a regime, called the "Orderly Liquidation Authority."[35] While critics oppose Title II for reasons beyond the scope of this report, proponents of the Dodd-Frank Act argue that eliminating the Fed's ability to prevent firms from failing under Section 13(3) will not result in financial instability now that firms can undergo an orderly resolution under Title II. According to Ben Bernanke, chairman of the Fed during the financial crisis, "With the creation of the [orderly] liquidation authority, the ability of the Fed to make loans to individual troubled firms like Bear [Stearns] and AIG was no longer needed and, appropriately, was eliminated."[36]

The Fed's Rule Implementing the Dodd-Frank Act's Changes

As Section 13(3) can be used only in "unusual and exigent circumstances" and had not been used for decades, the Fed had not promulgated a rule governing its use as of 2008, even though it had the discretion to do so. The Dodd-Frank Act also required the Fed to promulgate a rule implementing Section 1101 "as soon as is practicable," and the Fed issued a proposed rule doing so in 2013.[37] Some public comments criticized the rule for not adding meaningful quantitative or qualitative definitions to the terms "unusual and exigent circumstances," collateral, penalty rate, insolvency, broadly based, or the duration of assistance.[38] Generally, critics believe that the vagueness of the rule is undesirable for the same reason that proponents view it as desirable—because it maximize the Fed's future discretion.[39]

On December 18, 2015, the Fed promulgated a final rule implementing Section 1101.[40] Compared with the proposed rule, the final rule provided more specificity as to how the Fed would comply with the Dodd-Frank Act's requirements, and thus gives the Fed less discretion. For example, the final rule requires lending to be at a "penalty rate," which it defines as a premium to the market rate prevailing in normal circumstances. In some cases, the final rule goes beyond the statutory requirements. For example, statute only prohibits lending to firms that are in a bankruptcy or insolvency proceeding, whereas the final rule also prohibits lending to any facility unless it is open to at least five eligible borrowers, any recipient who has not been current on its debt over the past 90 days, a healthy firm for the purposes of preventing a third party from failing (as was the case with JP Morgan Chase and Bear Stearns), and a firm so that it can avoid bankruptcy or resolution. *Table 2* explains how the final rule implements the major provisions of Section 13(3).

Table 2. Major Provisions of the Fed's Final Rule Implementing Dodd-Frank Act Changes to Section 13(3)

Section 13(3) Provision	Final Rule Implementation
Limits assistance to any "participant in any program or facility with broad-based eligibility."	Minimum offive eligible participants for a program to meet the "broad-based eligibility" requirement.
Specifies that assistance be "for the purpose of providing liquidity to the financial system, and not to aid a failing financial company." Requires that	Specifies that liquidity may be provided only to an identifiable market or sector of the financial system. Provides that a program may not be used for a firm to

Section 13(3) Provision	Final Rule Implementation
regulations preclude insolvent borrowers, i.e., borrowers "in bankruptcy, resolution ... or any other Federal or State insolvency proceeding."	avoid bankruptcy or resolution. Specifies that a program designed to aid one or more failing companies or to assist one or more companies to avoid bankruptcy, resolution, or insolvency will not be considered to have the required "broad-based eligibility." Requires borrowers be current on their debt for 90 days before borrowing. Permits the Fed to determine whether the applicant is insolvent.Excludes a firm from borrowing from Fed if the purpose is to help a third-party firm that is insolvent. Includes immediate repayment and enforcement actions for firms that "make[s] a willful misrepresentation regarding its solvency." Specifies that the Fed is under no obligation to extend credit to a borrower.
Requires that loans be secured "sufficient[ly] to protect taxpayers from losses," and collateral be assigned a "lendable value" that is "consistent with sound risk management practices."	Requires that the Fed assign a lendable value to collateral at the time credit is extended.
Forbids "a program or facility that is structured to remove assets from thebalance sheet of a single and specific company."	Prohibits removing assets from one or more firms that meet the rule's definition of failing.
Requires "prior approval of the Secretary of the Treasury."	Specifies that no program may be established withouttheapproval of the Secretary of the Treasury.
Specifies that the authority may be invoked only in "unusual and exigent circumstances" and that any program be "terminated in a timely and orderly fashion."	Requires that the Fed provide "a description of the unusual and exigent circumstances that exist" no later than 7 days after establishing a program. Requires that initial credit terminate within one year, with extension possible only upon a vote of five governors and

Table 2. (Continued)

Section 13(3) Provision	Final Rule Implementation
	approval by the Secretary of the Treasury. Requires a review of programs every six months to assure timely termination.
Specifies that rates be consistent with the statutory requirements governing the discount rate.[a]	Requires the rate charged must be a "penalty rate," defined as a rate that is a premium to the market rate in normal circumstances. It must also be a rate that "affordsliquidity in unusual and exigent circumstances; and ... encourages repayment of the credit and discourages use of the program" when "economic conditions normalize." Permits the charging of "any fees, penalties,...or other consideration...to protect and appropriately compensate the taxpayer.... "
Specifies that the borrower must be "unable to secure adequate credit accommodations from other banking institutions."[a]	Requires evidence of inability of participants in a programto obtain credit. The evidence may be based on economic conditions in a particular market or markets; on the borrower's certification of its inability "to secure adequate credit accommodations from other banking institutions," or on "other evidence from participants or other sources."

Source: CRS based on Federal Reserve, "Extensions of Credit by Federal Reserve Banks," 80 Federal Register 78959, December 18, 2015, available at https://www.gpo.gov/fdsys/pkg/FR-2015-12-18/pdf/2015-30584.pdf.

[a] Requirement is largely unchanged by the Dodd-Frank Act.

Oversight Requirements

Following the use of Section 13(3) in 2008, three laws have been enacted affecting congressional oversight of emergency lending.

First, in 2008, Section 129 of the Emergency Economic Stabilization Act (P.L. 110-343) required the Fed to report to the congressional committees of jurisdiction on the terms of and justification for assistance within seven days of providing assistance under Section 13(3), with updates every 60 days.[41]

Second, in 2009, an amendment to the Helping Families Save Their Homes Act (Section 801 of P.L. 111-22) included a provision that allows Government Accountability Office (GAO) audits of "any action taken by the Board under ... Section 13(3) of the Federal Reserve Act with respect to a single and specific partnership or corporation." This provision allowed GAO audits of the Maiden Lane facilities and the asset guarantees of Citigroup and Bank of America, but it maintained audit restrictions on non-emergency activities and the broadly based emergency lending facilities.

Third, Section 1101 of the Dodd-Frank Act required that details on the assistance provided under Section 13(3) be reported to the committees of jurisdiction within seven days, with regular updates. Section 1103 required lending records (including details on the identity of the borrower and the terms of the loan) from the crisis to be publicly released on December 1, 2010,[42] and lending records from future programs created under Section 13(3) to be publicly released a year after the facility was terminated or two years after lending ceased, whichever came first. Section 1102 allowed GAO to audit any action under Section 13(3) for operational integrity, accounting, financial reporting, internal controls, effectiveness of collateral policies, favoritism, and use of third-party contractors—but did not allow GAO to conduct an economic evaluation—and Section 1109 required GAO to conduct an audit of all Fed emergency facilities created between December 2007 and enactment.[43] GAO may not disclose confidential information until the lending records are released.

For more details, see CRS Report R42079, *Federal Reserve: Oversight and Disclosure Issues*, by Marc Labonte.

POLICY ISSUES

Why Was the Fed Established as a "Lender of Last Resort"?

Economists distinguish between liquidity problems and solvency problems facing financial firms. Firms become insolvent when their assets are worth less than their liabilities (e.g., because their assets have fallen in value). Liquidity (i.e., cash flow) problems arise because of the maturity mismatch between a financial firm's long-term assets and short-term liabilities. In any instance where such a mismatch exists, no matter how much liquidity the firm holds, a firm is vulnerable to a loss of liquidity if it cannot roll over its short-term liabilities—even if the firm is solvent. In a crisis, creditors are unable to distinguish between solvent and insolvent firms, so both lose access to liquidity. The classic example of a liquidity crisis is a bank run, in which depositors withdraw their deposits (liabilities) and banks cannot liquidate loans (assets) to meet withdrawals. Holding more cash and fewer loans would make a run less likely but could not completely prevent it, and the unintended consequence would be that loans would be more expensive to customers. The Fed was created as a lender of last resort with this scenario in mind—when its depositors withdrew funds, a bank would be able to pledge its assets at the Fed's discount window in exchange for short-term loans. Because the Fed controls the money supply, it is in a unique position to potentially provide unlimited liquidity. This position enhances its ability to credibly pledge to end financial crises. Given that the Fed can only address liquidity problems, it is not equipped to address solvency problems or crises resulting from solvency problems, however.

One alternative to the Fed acting as a lender of last resort in a crisis is to allow the panic to run its course. This was the approach followed in the nineteenth and early twentieth centuries, until repeated panics resulted in the creation of the Fed. Eventually the panic would subside, but crises can lead to significant contractions in real economic activity and declines in prices. Crises cause economic contractions because financial firms extend less credit to consumers and businesses to hoard liquidity.

Who Should Have Access to the Lender of Last Resort?

Lending to Nonbank Financial Firms?

Do nonbank financial firms also face liquidity problems, and does this justify the Fed's emergency authority? Although only banks accept deposits, many types of financial firms face a maturity mismatch between long-term assets and short-term liabilities. As a result, many types of financial firms are vulnerable to liquidity crises. In 2008, the availability of repurchase agreements (repos) and commercial paper—two prominent types of short-term lending for nonbanks—sharply and suddenly contracted, causing liquidity problems for banks and nonfinancial firms. Thus, some nonbank financial firms could also benefit from access to Fed lending in a liquidity crisis.

Although some nonbank firms could benefit from access to a lender of last resort, policymakers might decide to grant them access only if there is some wider societal benefit to doing so. Such benefits could be because a failure to do so would result in financial instability, through spillover effects (e.g., counterparty exposure), contagion, or the disruption of critical functions within the financial system. Banks provide critical functions through their unique role in the payment system, for example. Nonbanks do not play a similar role in the payment system, although they are important participants in similar markets, such as the repo market, that might also be viewed as critical.[44]

Before 2008, there was some debate about whether nonbank financial firms were systemically important enough that there would be widespread repercussions if they faced a crisis. Likewise, there was some debate about whether a nonbank crisis would significantly affect the availability of credit to consumers and businesses. Over time, the nonbank financial sector has grown in absolute terms and relative to banks. The 2008 experience suggests that a nonbank crisis can be damaging to the availability of credit and the broader financial sector. Thus, the rationale of having a lender of last resort to provide liquidity also extends to parts of the nonbank financial system, although the policy tradeoffs may be different. This raises the question of whether there should be disparate treatment of banks and nonbanks—banks receive continual access to the discount window, whereas any given nonbank receives no access to the Fed in normal conditions and uncertain access to the Fed in unusual and exigent circumstances. Should nonbanks be allowed to be members of the Federal Reserve system to ensure access to the discount window?[45] If so, should they be subject to prudential supervision by the Fed?[46]

Not all uses of Section 13(3) during the crisis were for the purpose of providing short-term liquidity, however. TALF loans had terms of three to five years and were intended to revive longterm consumer and business credit (by increasing the demand for ABS, which might be described as increasing their liquidity). The AIG loan initially had a maturity of two years. The Maiden Lane facilities set up for Bear Stearns and AIG and the asset guarantees for Citigroup and Bank of America were all intended to help those firms with troubled assets. The Dodd-Frank Act now requires that assistance provided under Section 13(3) be "for the purpose of providing liquidity to the financial system, and not to aid a failing financial company."

Lending to Nonfinancial Firms?

Another issue is whether Section 13(3) should ever be used to provide credit to nonfinancial firms. In 2008, the Fed chose to use Section 13(3) to provide credit mainly to financial firms, although nonfinancial firms were eligible to sell their commercial paper to the CPFF. The Dodd-Frank Act limits actions under Section 13(3) to providing liquidity to the financial system, but does not limit participants to financial firms. In the 1930s, emergency loans were made to nonfinancial firms. Although nonfinancial firms might also have liquidity needs,[47] they do not generally face the maturity mismatch that makes liquidity risk inherent to financial firms. Liquidity problems at nonfinancial firms may also pose less systemic risk than at financial firms because they are less interconnected with the financial system and do not perform critical functions in the financial system.

The advantage of providing long-term credit to nonfinancial firms is that it directly stimulates physical capital investment spending on plant and equipment, which in turn directly stimulates gross domestic product (GDP). A disadvantage is that it is more likely to put the Fed in the position of "picking winners", and the Fed has no expertise in evaluating the creditworthiness of loan proposals. Another disadvantage is the potential that the Fed's lending will "crowd out" private capital. In a liquidity crisis, when the availability of private lending, by definition, is constrained, the likelihood that Fed lending comes at the expense of private lending is lower. By contrast, long-term credit, which will outlast a liquidity crisis, has a greater potential for crowding out.

Lending to Government or Government Chartered Entities?

Another category of firms that Congress might consider whether it wants to make ineligible for assistance under Section 13(3) is entities associated with the government, such as government agencies, government-sponsored enterprises (GSEs), or bridge banks created in an FDIC resolution.[48] Some Members of Congress have also expressed concern that Section 13(3) could be used to assist state or municipal governments. The Fed has never used Section 13(3) for these purposes, although it has purchased agency and GSE debt under its normal authority. Current statute does not explicitly rule it out, although such an action might have trouble meeting the statute's various requirements, such as that the facility be broadly based for the purpose of providing liquidity to the financial system.

Lending to Itself?

During the crisis, the Fed structured many of its transactions under Section 13(3) as loans to a LLC that it created and controlled. It did so to comply with the Section 13(3) requirement that assistance take the form of a loan. For example, in 2008, the Fed created the Commercial Paper Funding Facility (CPFF) to purchase commercial paper, a debt security that is economically equivalent to a short-term loan from the borrower's perspective. In this case, the Fed was able to purchase commercial paper by setting up a limited liability corporation (LLC) that it controlled and lending the LLC funds to finance the purchases. Some of the commercial paper the CPFF purchased was not collateralized, however, so it was not economically equivalent to a collateralized loan.

These actions raise two policy issues. First, should Section 13(3) be restricted so that the Fed cannot lend to LLCs it creates and controls? Second, should Section 13(3) be modified so that the Fed can provide short-term liquidity by purchasing debt securities?[49]

From an economic perspective, whether a company accesses short-term liquidity by taking out a loan or issuing a debt security does not change its purpose. On practical grounds, since financial firms increasingly rely on debt securities for liquidity needs, allowing the Fed to purchase them would make it a more effective lender of last resort. But allowing the Fed to purchase securities (directly or through LLCs it controls) to provide short-term liquidity faces the "slippery slope" problem. The Fed also used LLCs in the Maiden Lanes case, where the goal was not to provide short-term liquidity but to remove troubled assets from a firm's balance sheet. The Dodd-Frank Act maintained the Fed's ability to create LLCs, but prohibits "a program or facility that is structured to remove assets from the balance sheet of a single and specific company." It might be difficult to draw a bright line between debt securities purchased for liquidity purposes and other types of securities.

What Are the Potential Costs of Emergency Assistance?

Potential costs inherent in Section 13(3) lending can be divided into risks to taxpayers and broader economic consequences. These costs can be weighed against the benefits of Section 13(3) lending, which could be significant if the lending restores or maintains financial stability. While lending poses risks to the taxpayer, if the Fed did not act, the economic losses from allowing a financial crisis to run its course would also pose risks to taxpayers in terms of a larger federal budget deficit and privately through higher unemployment, lost wealth, and so forth.

The risk to the taxpayer of lending is primarily default risk. The Fed can— but is not required to— attach various conditions to its lending to minimize default, including requiring short maturities, collateral in excess of the funds lent (i.e., applying a "haircut" to collateral), senior creditor standing, and recourse if collateral proves insufficient. Note that the Fed has typically—but not always—imposed all of these conditions to Section 13(3) assistance. Loans to nonbanks are arguably not inherently riskier than loans to banks; to the extent that Section 13(3) programs were riskier than the discount window, it was mainly because these conditions were loosened. Lending to non-banks may also be riskier because the Fed can safeguard its lending to banks through prudential supervision, but, with the exception of firms designated as "systemically important financial institutions" (SIFIs) or structured as bank holding companies, the Fed has no jurisdiction to supervise nonbanks for safety and soundness. In times of crisis, the Fed's broader ability to restore financial stability also reduces default risk for any specific loan.

In some cases, the Fed was able to protect the taxpayer through terms other than conventional collateral pledges. For example, the Fed required that AIG provide it with compensation in the form of an equity stake in the company in exchange for a loan. The Fed's ability to protect taxpayers against losses could be more limited in the future based on a recent court ruling. The court found that the AIG equity stake was an illegal exaction.[50] However, because the Dodd-Frank Act prohibits assistance to single or failing firms, future scenarios in which the Fed would need to take an equity stake to adequately protect taxpayers may be limited.

One broader economic concern with Section 13(3) lending raised by House Financial Services Committee Chairman Jeb Hensarling is that "its use risks exacerbating moral hazard costs."[51] Moral hazard is the concept that firms will take greater risks if they are protected from negative outcomes. In this case, moral hazard occurs because firms are more likely to be more reliant on short-term lending if they anticipate access to Fed lending during a liquidity crisis. Some argue that Section 13(3) should be repealed or curbed because of moral hazard, but Bernanke compares that approach to shutting down the fire department to encourage fire safety, instead of toughening the fire code.[52] Unlike lending to banks, the Fed cannot mitigate moral hazard through prudential supervision, however, except in the cases noted above.

Moral hazard concerns can be overstated. For instance, moral hazard arguably did not cause nonbank financial firms to be reckless about liquidity management before the crisis, unless they were able to anticipate that Section 13(3) would be used to provide them with liquidity, even though it had never been used for that purpose before 2008. Thus, greater market discipline might reduce moral hazard problems but cannot eliminate liquidity crises.

How Much Discretion Should the Fed Be Granted?

Limiting discretion is the common goal running throughout many of the diverse policy proposals to alter Section 13(3). The fact that the Fed has broad discretion under Section 13(3) allowed the Fed, for or better or worse, to act swiftly, pledge sizable funds, create a diverse set of facilities for a diverse set of lenders, and tackle multiple, disparate problems as they emerged. It also explains why the Fed was able to provide assistance in forms not envisioned by Congress that arguably were not always consistent with the spirit of a lender of last resort, such as the Maiden Lane LLCs.[53]

One potential drawback to discretion is that assistance might be provided in ways the Dodd-Frank Act did not intend, such as to prevent a firm from failing. As noted above, the Dodd-Frank Act modified Section 13(3) to rule out lending to an insolvent firm, but some critics are skeptical that the Dodd-Frank Act successfully ruled out the use of Section 13(3) to aid an insolvent firm. The Fed's final rule further limits its ability to assist a failing firm by prohibiting the creation of any facility unless it is open to at least five eligible borrowers, lending to any recipient who is not current on debt over the past 90 days, lending to a healthy firm for the purposes of preventing a third party from failing (as was the case with JP Morgan Chase and Bear Stearns), and lending to a firm so that it can avoid bankruptcy or resolution. Nevertheless, as long as emergency authority exists, policymakers may be tempted to use it to bail out a failing firm to avoid a crisis—and the broader the authority, the more feasible it becomes.[54]

Arguably, another drawback to discretion is the potential for favoritism. Because the types of nonbank financial firms are numerous and diverse, deciding who should get access to loans involves trade-offs and judgments that are not completely technical in nature. For example, the Fed set a high minimum loan size in TALF that effectively limited access to loans at below-market interest rates to large investors. The decision to outsource certain functions of emergency facilities to third-party vendors also creates the potential for favoritism.[55]

Another consideration for the degree of discretion provided is the Fed's independence from Congress and the Administration. The Fed argues that maintaining its independence is important for the credibility and effectiveness of its monetary policy. At the same time, greater independence complicates accountability to Congress. It is fair to question to what degree limiting discretion on Section 13(3) affects perceptions of monetary policy independence because 13(3) is used so rarely. The Dodd-Frank Act's requirement that assistance under Section 13(3) be preapproved by the Treasury Secretary reduces the Fed's independence from the Administration, although the Treasury Secretary supported all of the Fed's actions taken under Section 13(3) in 2008.

Fed governor Jerome Powell believes that the Congress should maintain the Fed's current discretion under Section 13(3) because

> One of the lessons of the crisis is that the financial system evolves so quickly that it is difficult to predict where threats will emerge and what actions may be needed in the future to respond. Because we cannot anticipate what may be needed in the future, the Congress should preserve the ability of the Fed to respond flexibly and nimbly to future emergencies. Further restricting or eliminating the Fed's emergency lending authority will not prevent future crises, but it will hinder the Fed's ability to limit the harm from those crises for families and businesses.[56]

Alternatively, some argue that discretion can increase uncertainty, thereby increasing systemic risk. For example, some argue that the failure of Lehman Brothers exacerbated financial instability because market participants believed that it would receive Fed assistance similar to Bear Stearns and panicked when it did not.

The Dodd-Frank Act reduced the Fed's discretion under Section 13(3), and the final rule implementing those changes reduced it further. In Governor Powell's view, the Dodd-Frank reforms "struck a reasonable balance ... (and) it would be a mistake to go further and impose additional restrictions" on Section 13(3). By reducing the Fed's discretion, Chair Janet Yellen has stated that H.R. 3189 would "essentially repeal the Federal Reserve's remaining ability to act in a crisis."[57] By contrast, Chairman Hensarling believes that "Dodd-Frank tried but failed to rein in the Fed's emergency lending authority."[58]

Congress could curb discretion by adding more restrictions to Section 13(3) or by requiring Congressional approval for each action taken under Section 13(3). The latter proposal, depending on the details, could potentially affect the timeliness and credibility of the Fed's actions during a crisis. Examples of additional restrictions Congress could add to Section 13(3) include restrictions on who is eligible for assistance and the terms of assistance, such as acceptable collateral or the rate that the Fed charges (discussed below). Congress could also add limits on the amount of total assistance or assistance to one borrower.[59] Granting the Fed discretion on these issues is in part a judgment by Congress about whether it or the Fed can balance these competing policy considerations more effectively. For example, favoritism concerns could potentially be exacerbated or mitigated if Congress were more involved.

What Rate Should the Fed Charge?

In determining what rate the lender of last resort should charge, economists and central bankers almost universally point to the maxim of Walter Bagehot—lend freely against good collateral, but at a penalty.[60] Consensus breaks down on how penurious the penalty rate should be. A penalty rate (i.e., a rate that is higher than the market rate) achieves two goals: (1) it maximizes the return to the central bank (and thus the taxpayer) and (2) it discourages lenders from turning to the central bank instead of the private market when private credit is available (hence, the concept of lender of *last* resort), thereby reducing moral hazard problems. These two goals call for making the rate as high as possible. Alternatively, financial stability concerns call for making the rate as close to market rates as possible. Higher rates will potentially undermine financial stability by discouraging the use of Fed facilities, which may increase the stigma associated with borrowing from the Fed (i.e., if lending is made unattractive to healthy firms, the decision to borrow could be taken as a sign of desperation). Further, higher rates might weaken the health of the borrower, thereby undermining the goal of restoring stability. This concept is most starkly demonstrated in the case of assistance to AIG during the crisis (for details, see the *Appendix*). The terms of the initial Fed loan were more favorable to the taxpayer than the subsequent iterations of assistance, which were repeatedly renegotiated for fear that overly harsh terms would compromise the company's viability.

There is also a question of how a market rate should be calculated during a crisis. Generally, two features of a crisis are that markets become illiquid (so there are fewer transactions to observe) and rates become higher. These features would argue for using a pre-crisis market rate as the baseline. Critics incorrectly accused the Fed of charging below-market rates during the crisis.[61] The seeming contradiction between the low rates charged by the Fed in absolute terms and the fact that these rates were a markup above market rates is explained by the fact that the market rates referenced by the Fed were directly influenced by monetary policy. At the same time the Fed was making these loans, it was in the process of reducing the federal funds rate to zero.

The possibility of a limited group of recipients receiving below-market borrowing rates was arguably greatest in the two cases in which the direct recipients of the loans were not the intended recipients of ultimate assistance. The AMLF made loans to banks to finance the purchase of commercial paper to relieve stress in the commercial-paper market. The TALF made loans to investment funds to purchase ABS to revive the private-securitization market. Borrowers would only choose to participate in these programs if they could reasonably expect that, adjusted for risk, the profits they would earn from the purchase of commercial paper or ABS would exceed the interest on Fed loans. To entice banks and investors, respectively, to participate in these programs, the Fed made the terms of the programs relatively attractive to them (e.g., the loans were non-recourse), potentially reducing the profits and increasing the risk exposure for the Fed. Weighed against these costs, this arrangement may have had benefits to the Fed, such as avoiding the need to "pick winners" or develop the financial expertise to accurately price complex securities.

Section 13(3) does not address whether a penalty rate should be charged, but the final rule implementing the Dodd-Frank Act's modifications requires the Fed to charge a penalty rate, defined as a premium to the market rate prevailing in normal circumstances.

Should Borrowers' Identities Be Kept Confidential?

Many Members of Congress contend that taxpayers have a right to know to whom the Fed is lending and on what terms because taxpayers are the ultimate backstop for these loans. The Fed has argued that allowing the public to know which firms are accessing its facilities could undermine investor confidence in the institutions receiving aid because of a perception that recipients are weak or unsound. A loss of investor confidence could potentially lead to destabilizing runs on the institution's deposits, debt, or equity. If institutions feared that this would occur, the Fed argues, the institutions would be wary of participating in the Fed's programs. A delayed release of information mitigates, but does not eliminate, these concerns. Some critics would view less Fed lending as a positive outcome, but if the premise that the Fed's lender of last resort role helps prevent financial crises by maintaining the liquidity of the financial system is accepted, then an unwillingness by institutions to access Fed facilities makes the system less safe. One study argues that the Fed's decision to discourage banks to use the discount window from 1929-1931 (at a time when identities were kept confidential) worsened the bank panic in the Great Depression.[62]

Whether investors are less willing to borrow as a result of the disclosure of identities will not be apparent until the next crisis. A historical example supporting the Fed's argument would be the experience with the Reconstruction Finance Corporation (RFC) in the Great Depression. When the RFC publicized to which banks it had given loans, those banks typically experienced depositor runs.[63] A more recent example—disclosure of TARP fund recipients—provides mixed evidence. At first, TARP funds were widely disbursed, and recipients included all the major banks. At that point, there was no perceived stigma to TARP participation. Subsequently, many banks repaid TARP shares at the first opportunity, and several remaining participants have expressed concern that if they did not repay soon, investors would perceive them as weak.

The granularity of information to be disclosed is a policy issue. Aggregate information about programs and activities that does not require the identification of borrowers tends to be more useful for broad policy purposes, while current information on specific transactions within the programs is of interest to investors. The Fed voluntarily released the former, but only reluctantly released the latter when compelled to by legislation and lawsuits. For oversight purposes, the former would suffice for answering most questions about taxpayer risk exposure, expected profits or losses, potential subsidies, economic effects, and evaluating the state of the financial system. The latter would be necessary for transparency around issues such as favoritism (certain firms receiving preferential treatment over similar firms).[64] Although preventing favoritism is a valid policy goal, releasing the identities of borrowers to "name and shame" them is more questionable, especially if one believes that these programs were helpful for providing liquidity and maintaining financial stability. Naming and shaming is likely to result in less uptake of the programs in the future. If one believes that these lending programs are not helpful, repealing Section 13(3) would be more effective than undermining their effectiveness by stigmatizing recipients.

As discussed above, the Dodd-Frank Act compromised between stability and oversight concerns by requiring borrowers' identities to be publicly released with a lag. Some Members of Congress have expressed an interest in revisiting this issue.

SELECTED LEGISLATION IN THE 114TH CONGRESS

H.R. 3189

The Fed Oversight Reform and Modernization Act (H.R. 3189) was ordered to be reported by the House Financial Services Committee on July 29, 2015. On November 19, 2015, it was passed by the House. Section 11 of the bill as passed amends Section 13(3) to limit the Fed's discretion to make emergency loans. It would limit 13(3) to "unusual and exigent circumstances that pose a threat to the financial stability of the United States" and would require "the affirmative vote of not less than nine presidents of Federal reserve banks" in addition to the current requirement of the affirmative vote of five Fed governors. It would forbid the Fed from accepting as collateral equity securities issued by a borrower. It would require the Fed to issue a rule establishing how it would determine sufficiency of collateral; acceptable classes of collateral; any discount that would be applied to determine the sufficiency of collateral; and how it would obtain independent appraisals for valuing collateral. It would eliminate the current language permitting the Fed to establish the solvency of a borrower based on the borrower's certification and would specify that before a borrower may be eligible for assistance, the Fed's Board and any other federal banking regulator with jurisdiction over the borrower must certify that the borrower is not insolvent. It would limit assistance to institutions "predominantly engaged in financial activities" and preclude assistance to federal, state, and local government agencies and government-controlled or sponsored entities. It would require the Fed to issue a rule establishing a minimum interest rate on emergency loans based on the sum of the average secondary discount rate charged by the Federal Reserve banks over the most recent 90-day period and the average of the difference between a distressed corporate bond index (as defined by a rule issued by the Fed) and the Treasury yield over the most recent 90-day period.

S. 1320

The Bailout Prevention Act (S. 1320) would amend Section 13(3) to limit the Fed's discretion to make emergency loans. It eliminates the current language permitting the Fed to establish the solvency of a borrower based on the borrower's certification and specifies that a borrower may not be eligible for assistance unless the Fed and all federal banking regulators with jurisdiction over the borrower certify that the borrower is not insolvent and issue a detailed public explanation of the certification decision. The certification must be based on an assessment of "relevant financial data" for the most recent four months and determine that the fair value of the borrower's assets exceeds the fair value of liabilities—adjusting for temporary market illiquidity. It forbids the Fed from lending to a bridge company set up under Title II of the Dodd-Frank Act. It defines broad-based eligibility to comprise at least five companies. Its sets the minimum interest rate on a loan to be at least five percentage points above the yield on a Treasury security with a comparable duration. It provides the Fed with authority to create a program that does not meet the bill's definition of broad-based eligibility or minimum lending rate, provided it notifies Congress within three days. If a joint resolution authorizing the program to continue is not enacted within 30 days of receipt of that notice, the program terminates. Section 4 of the bill is unrelated to Fed emergency lending.

H.R. 2625

The Bailout Prevention Act (H.R. 2625) would amend Section 13(3) to limit the Fed's discretion to make emergency loans. It eliminates the current language permitting the Fed to establish the solvency of a borrower based on the borrower's certification and specifies that a borrower may not be eligible for assistance unless the Fed and all federal banking regulators with jurisdiction over the borrower certify that the borrower is not insolvent and issue a detailed public explanation of the certification decision. The certification must be based on an assessment of "relevant financial data" for the most recent four months and determine that the fair value of the borrower's assets exceeds the fair value of liabilities—adjusting for temporary market illiquidity. It forbids the Fed from lending to a bridge company set up under Title II of the Dodd-Frank Act. It defines broad-based eligibility to comprise at least five companies. Its sets the minimum interest rate on a loan to be at least five percentage points above the yield on a Treasury security with a comparable duration. It provides the Fed with authority to create a program that does not meet the bill's definition of broad-based eligibility or minimum lending rate, provided it notifies Congress within three days. If a joint resolution authorizing the program to continue is not enacted within 30 days of receipt of that notice, the program terminates. It would reduce the delayed release of unredacted GAO reports and lending records pertaining to Section 13(3) from one or two years to 60 days.

Appendix. Details on the Actions Taken under Section 13(3) in 2008

Term Securities Lending Facility

Shortly before Bear Stearns suffered its liquidity crisis, the Fed created the Term Securities Lending Facility (TSLF) on March 11, 2008, to expand its existing securities lending program for primary dealers.[65] Primary dealers are financial firms that are the Fed's counterparties for open market operations, including investment banks that were ineligible to access the Fed's lending facilities for banks. At the end of 2007, there were 20 primary dealers, including Bear Stearns.[66] The proximate cause of Bear Stearns' crisis was its inability to roll over its short-term debt, and the Fed created the TSLF and the Primary Dealer Credit Facility (discussed below) to offer an alternative source of short-term liquidity for primary dealers.

Primary dealers were already allowed to borrow securities from the Fed on an overnight basis before the crisis. The TSLF extended the length of the loans and acceptable collateral, and signaled that the Fed was willing to lend on a larger scale. Under the TSLF at its peak, each week primary dealers could borrow up to $200 billion of Treasury securities for 28 days, as opposed to overnight. Primary dealers need access to Treasury securities because of their use in repurchase agreements (repos), which are an important source of short-term financing. *Figure A-1* shows the decline in primary dealer repos outstanding in 2008. At various points, loans could be collateralized with some of the following: private-label mortgage-backed securities (MBS) with an AAA/Aaa rating, agency commercial MBS, agency collateralized mortgage obligations, and all investment-grade debt securities. On July 30, 2008, the Fed created the TSLF Options Program within the TSLF that allowed primary dealers to pre-negotiate options to borrow securities. No securities were borrowed through the TSLF after August 2009, and the facility expired February 1, 2010. The TSLF experienced no losses and earned income of $781 million over the life of the program.

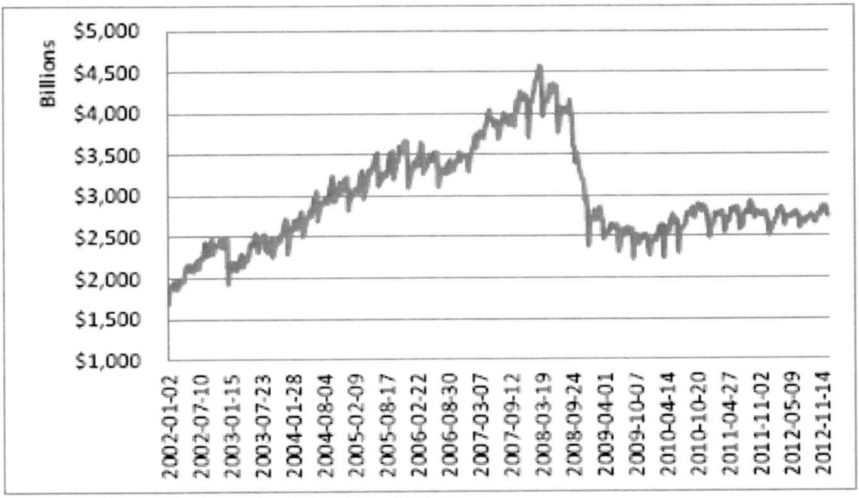

Source: New York Fed, Primary Dealer Statistics.
Note: Includes overnight, continuing, and term agreement repos

Figure A- I I. Primary Dealer Repos Outstanding (2002-2012, weekly)

Primary Dealer Credit Facility

Shortly after Bear Stearns' liquidity crisis, the Fed created the Primary Dealer Credit Facility (PDCF) on March 16, 2008. The PDCF can be thought of as analogous to a discount window for primary dealers.[67] Loans were made at the Fed's discount rate, which was set slightly higher than the federal funds rate during the crisis. Loans were made on an overnight basis, with recourse, and they were fully collateralized, limiting their riskiness. Acceptable collateral at times included Treasuries; government agency debt; investment grade corporate, mortgage-backed, asset-backed, and municipal securities; and certain classes of equities. The PDCF expired on February 1, 2010.

Borrowing from the facility was sporadic, with average daily borrowing outstanding above $10 billion in the first three months and falling to zero in August 2008. Much of this initial borrowing was done by Bear Stearns, before its merger with JPMorgan Chase was complete. Borrowing picked up again in September 2008 and peaked at $148 billion on October 1, 2008. No loans were outstanding after May 2009. The PDCF experienced no losses and earned interest income of $0.5 billion over the life of the program.

Commercial Paper Funding Facility and Asset-Backed Commercial Paper Money Market Mutual Fund Liquidity Facility

To meet liquidity needs, many large firms routinely issue commercial paper, which is short-term debt purchased directly by investors that matures in less than 270 days, with an average maturity of 30 days. The three broad categories of commercial paper issuers are financial firms, nonfinancial firms, and pass-through entities that issue commercial paper backed by assets. The commercial paper issued directly by firms tends not to be backed by collateral, because these firms are viewed as large and creditworthy, and the paper matures quickly.

Individual investors are major purchasers of highly rated commercial paper through money market mutual funds (MMMFs) and money market accounts. On September 16, 2008, a MMMF called the Reserve Fund "broke the buck," meaning that the value of its shares had fallen below par value of $1. This occurred because of losses it had taken on short-term debt issued by Lehman Brothers, which filed for bankruptcy on September 15, 2008. Money market investors had perceived breaking the buck to be highly unlikely, and its occurrence set off a generalized run on MMMFs, as investors simultaneously attempted to withdraw an estimated $250 billion of their investments—even from funds without exposure to Lehman.[68] The decline in commercial paper outstanding after September 2008 is illustrated in *Figure A-2*.

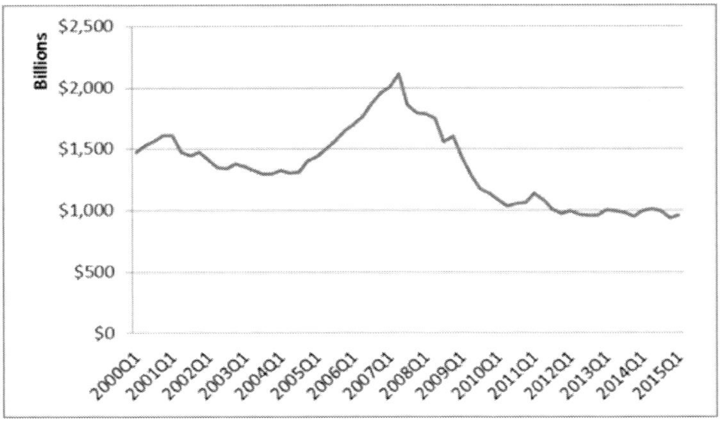

Source: Federal Reserve, Z.1 release.

Figure A-2. Commercial Paper Outstanding. (2000:Q1-2015:Q1, quarterly).

Fearing that disruption in the commercial paper markets could make overall problems in financial markets more severe, the Fed announced on September 19, 2008, that it would create the Asset-Backed Commercial Paper Money Market Mutual Fund Liquidity Facility (AMLF). This facility made nonrecourse loans to banks to purchase asset-backed commercial paper. As the commercial paper matured, the loans were repaid. Because the loans were nonrecourse, the banks had no further liability to repay any losses on the commercial paper collateralizing the loan. At its peak in early October 2008, the AMLF had loans of $152 billion outstanding. However, the AMLF would soon be superseded in importance by the creation of the Commercial Paper Funding Facility (CPFF), and lending fell to zero in October 2009. The AMLF experienced no losses and earned income of $0.5 billion over the life of the program. The facility expired on February 1, 2010.

On October 7, 2008, the Fed announced the creation of the CPFF to purchase all types of three-month, highly rated U.S. commercial paper, secured and unsecured, from issuers.[69] The CPFF charged an interest rate equal to the three-month overnight index swap rate plus 1 percentage point for secured corporate debt, 2 percentage points for unsecured corporate debt, and 3 percentage points for asset-backed paper. The CPFF could buy as much commercial paper from any individual issuer as that issuer had outstanding in the year to date. Any potential losses borne by the CPFF would ultimately be borne by the Fed. At its peak in January 2009, the CPFF held $351 billion of commercial paper, and holdings fell steadily subsequently. The facility expired February 1, 2010. It earned income of $6.1 billion over the life of the program and suffered no losses.

In the case of the AMLF, the banks were not intended recipients of assistance, but rather were the intermediary through which assistance flowed to the commercial paper market. According to GAO, 92% of credit extended under AMLF was channeled through two custodial banks (JPMorgan Chase and State Street) that were among the three largest providers of fund administration and account services for MMMFs.[70] The CPFF removed the role of banks as intermediary and provided Fed assistance directly to commercial paper issuers.[71]

On October 21, 2008, the Fed announced the creation of the Money Market Investor Funding Facility (MMIFF) and pledged to lend it up to $540 billion. The MMIFF was planned to lend to private-sector special purpose vehicles (SPVs) that invest in commercial paper issued by highly rated financial institutions. Each SPV would have been owned by a group of financial firms and could only purchase commercial paper issued by that group. The intent was for these SPVs to purchase commercial paper from money market mutual funds and similar entities facing redemption requests to help avoid runs, such as the run on the Reserve Fund. The MMIFF was never accessed, and the facility expired on October 30, 2009.

Term Asset-Backed Securities Loan Facility

On November 25, 2008, the Fed created the Term Asset-Backed Securities Loan Facility (TALF) in response to problems in the market for asset-backed securities (ABS).[72] According to the Fed, "new issuance of ABS declined precipitously in September and came to a halt in October. At the same time, interest rate spreads on AAA-rated tranches of ABS soared to levels well outside the range of historical experience, reflecting unusually high risk premiums."[73] The decline in ABS issuance is illustrated in *Figure A-3*. The Fed feared that if lenders could not securitize these types of loans, less credit would be extended to consumers, exacerbating the economic downturn.

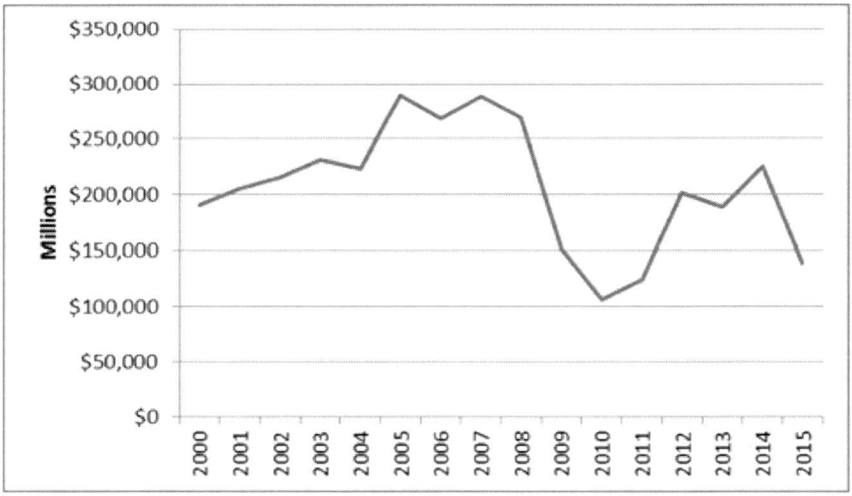

Source: Securities Industry and Financial Markets Association, data accessed at http://www.sifma.org/uploadedFiles/Research/Statistics/StatisticsFiles/SF-US-ABS-SIFMA.xls?n=55152.

Note: Does not include mortgage-backed securities.

Figure A-3. Asset-Backed Securities Issuance. (2000-2015, annually).

Rather than purchase ABS directly, the Fed made nonrecourse loans to private investment funds to purchase recently issued ABS with the highest credit rating, using the ABS as collateral. The minimum loan size was $10 million. Eligible collateral included new securities backed by auto loans, student loans, small business loans, and credit card loans. TALF was later expanded to include "legacy" commercial MBS. The loans had a term of up to three years for most types of assets (and up to five years for some types of assets), but were repaid when the underlying ABS matured or was sold. Interest rates were set at a markup over different maturities of the London Interbank Offered Rate (LIBOR) or the federal funds rate, depending on the type of loan and underlying collateral.

If the ABS had lost value, because the loans were nonrecourse, the losses would have been borne by the Fed and the Treasury (through TARP) instead of by the borrower—an unusual feature that made TALF riskier for taxpayers than typical Fed lending facilities. The Fed lent less than the market value of the collateral, so the Fed would not have borne losses on the loans until losses exceeded the value of this "haircut" (different ABS receive different haircuts). In addition, Treasury initially set aside $20 billion of TARP funds to cover any losses.[74]

Peaking at $48 billion, TALF turned out to be a relatively small program compared with the $200 billion program envisioned by the Fed or the $1 trillion program later envisioned by Treasury. In part, this was because the issuance of assets eligible for TALF remained low, which reflected the depressed state of securitization markets and may imply that TALF was unable to overcome investor aversion to ABS. (While TALF was in operation beginning in March 2009, a sizable share of ABS issued were used as collateral for TALF loans. Thus, issuance might have been even lower without the presence of TALF.)

Unlike most other Fed lending facilities, the amount outstanding under TALF steadily rose through 2009. The facility stopped making new loans at the end of June 2010 for loans using newly issued commercial MBS as collateral and in March 2010 for loans using other assets. The last TALF loan was repaid on October 29, 2014. All TALF loans were repaid in full, with interest.[75] Over the life of the program, TALF made profits of $1.6 billion for the Fed and $0.7 billion for the Treasury.

Bear Stearns

Unable to roll over its short-term debt as a result of investor concerns about its mortgage-related losses, the investment bank Bear Stearns faced bankruptcy in 2008. Fearing that Bear Stearns was "too big to fail" and posed systemic risk,[76] the Fed stepped in to broker a merger. On March 14, 2008, the Fed provided a $12.9 billion bridge loan on a nonrecourse basis to JP Morgan Chase to provide Bear Stearns with liquidity, which was repaid with interest. On March 16, JPMorgan Chase agreed to acquire Bear Stearns. As part of the agreement, the Fed agreed to lend $28.82 billion to Maiden Lane I, a Delaware limited liability corporation (LLC) that it created, to purchase financial securities at market value from Bear Stearns. These securities were largely mortgage-related assets that were too illiquid for JPMorgan Chase to be willing to acquire.

Maiden Lane I, not JP Morgan Chase, was to repay the Fed interest and principal using the funds from the sale of the assets. JP Morgan Chase took a first loss position through a subordinated loan of $1.15 billion, receiving an interest rate of 4.5% above the discount rate on that position, compared with an interest rate of 2.5% above the discount rate on the Fed's loan. Any additional losses would be borne by the Fed, and any profits in excess of the loans would accrue to the Fed. Profits or losses for the Fed and JP Morgan Chase were dependent on whether the market value of those assets rose or declined after Maiden Lane I acquired them.

By November 2012, proceeds from the sale or maturation of Maiden Lane I assets were sufficient to fully repay principal and accrued interest to the Fed ($765 million) and JP Morgan Chase. As of December 30, 2014, the value of remaining assets held by Maiden Lane I was $1.7 billion.[77] Once those remaining assets are sold or have matured, the Fed will realize additional capital gains that would be greater or less than $1.7 billion (less expenses), depending on whether the value of those assets subsequently rises or falls.

American International Group

In September 2008, facing losses on various operations, AIG experienced a significant decline in its stock price and downgrades from the major credit rating agencies.[78] These downgrades led to immediate demands for significant amounts of collateral (approximately $14 billion to $15 billion in collateral payments, according to contemporary press reports).[79] As financial demands on the company mounted, bankruptcy appeared a possibility, as had occurred with Lehman Brothers on September 15, 2008. Many feared that AIG was too big to fail due to the potential for widespread disruption to financial markets resulting from such a failure.

On September 16, 2008 (prior to the existence of TARP), the Fed announced that it was taking action to support AIG in the form of a secured two-year line of credit with a value of up to $85 billion and an interest rate of 8.5 percentage points above the three-month LIBOR. In addition, the government received warrants to purchase up to 79.9% of the equity in AIG. On October 8, 2008, the Fed announced that it would lend AIG up to an additional $37.8 billion against securities held by its insurance subsidiaries.[80]

In early November 2008 (following the creation of TARP), the financial support for AIG was restructured. The restructured financial support consisted of (1) reducing the size of the Fed loan to up to $60 billion, with the term lengthened to five years and the interest rate reduced by 5.5 percentage points; (2) purchasing $40 billion in preferred shares through TARP; and (3) replacing the $37.8 billion loan with up to $52.5 billion total in asset purchases by the Fed through two LLCs known as Maiden Lane II and Maiden Lane III. The 79.9% equity position of the government in AIG remained essentially unchanged after the restructuring of the intervention.

In March 2009, the assistance was restructured further through (1) a partial payback of the Fed loan through a swap of debt for equity in two AIG subsidiaries worth approximately $25 billion, reducing the maximum to $35 billion and (2) commitments for additional future TARP purchases of up to $29.8 billion in preferred shares at AIG's discretion, and the conversion of existing shares into shares with optional dividend payments.[81] The Maiden Lane LLCs continued operating under the previous terms, with the actual loans extended to the LLCs totaling $43.9 billion at their peak.

In September 2010, AIG and the government announced another restructuring of the government's assistance. This restructuring closed on January 14, 2011. The expressed goal was to simplify the government's interest in AIG and provide a path for the government to divest its stake in AIG. The essence of the plan called for (1) ending the Fed's involvement with AIG through loan repayment and transfer of the Fed's equity interests to Treasury and (2) converting the government's $49.1 billion in existing preferred shares into common shares, which could then be sold to the public over time. The specific steps involved several interlocking transactions, including the initial public offering of a large AIG subsidiary, the sale of several other AIG subsidiaries, and the use of up to approximately $20 billion in TARP funds to transfer equity interests from the Fed to the Treasury.

All of the Fed loans have been repaid, and the assets held in the Maiden Lane LLCs have been sold. Maiden Lanes II and III were formally terminated on November 12, 2014. The Fed earned interest of $8.2 billion on the loan to AIG and $9.5 billion on the Maiden Lanes. In addition to the income received by the Fed, Treasury received an additional $17.6 billion on the sale of equity that the Fed originally received (and subsequently transferred to the Treasury) as recompense for the Fed's loan to AIG.

Citigroup

On November, 23, 2008, the Treasury, Fed, and Federal Deposit Insurance Corporation (FDIC) announced a joint intervention in Citigroup, which had previously received $25 billion in TARP Capital Purchase Program funding.[82] This exceptional intervention to "[support] financial stability" consisted of an additional $20 billion purchase of preferred shares through the TARP Targeted Investment Program and a government guarantee for a pool of $306 billion in Citigroup assets (reduced to $301 billion when the guarantee was finalized on January 16, 2009) through the TARP Asset Guarantee Program, the FDIC, and the Fed.[83]

In December 2009, Citigroup and Treasury reached an agreement to cancel the asset guarantee. While the asset guarantee was in place, no losses were claimed and no federal funds were paid out. The Fed's share of the termination fee for the asset guarantee was $50 million.[84]

Bank of America

On January 16, 2009, the Treasury, Fed, and FDIC announced a joint intervention in Bank of America, which had previously received $25 billion in TARP Capital Purchase Program funds. Bank of America's losses were largest at Merrill Lynch, which it was in the process of taking over. The Fed and Treasury may have been most concerned that if Bank of America was not offered special assistance, the merger would fall through and Merrill Lynch would experience a disorderly failure. "[A]s part of its commitment to support financial market stability,"[85] this exceptional assistance included the purchase of an additional $20 billion of Bank of America preferred shares through the

TARP Targeted Investment Program and a joint guarantee on a pool of up to $118 billion of certain Bank of America assets (largely those acquired through its merger with Merrill Lynch). The announced guarantee was to remain in place for 10 years for residential mortgage-related assets and 5 years for all other assets. Bank of America would have borne up to the first $10 billion of losses on the assets, with subsequent losses split 90% to the government and 10% to Bank of America. Within the government, the losses were to be split between the TARP Asset Guarantee Program, the FDIC, and the Fed.

Although the asset guarantee was announced in January 2009, a final agreement was never signed. On September 21, 2009, Bank of America announced that it had negotiated a $425 million termination fee (of which, the Fed received $57 million) that allowed it to withdraw from the Asset Guarantee Program.[86]

End Notes

[1] David Fettig, Lender of More than Last Resort, Federal Reserve Bank of Minneapolis, December 1, 2002, https://www.minneapolisfed.org/publications/the-region/lender-of-more-than-last-resort.

[2] For more information, see CRS Report RL30354, Monetary Policy and the Federal Reserve: Current Policy and Conditions, by Marc Labonte.

[3] For an overview, see CRS Report R43413, Costs of Government Interventions in Response to the Financial Crisis: A Retrospective, by Baird Webel and Marc Labonte.

[4] Howard Hackley, Lending Functions of the Federal Reserve Banks, Federal Reserve, 1973, p. 130. See also David Fettig, Lender of More than Last Resort, Federal Reserve Bank of Minneapolis, December 1, 2002, https://www.minneapolisfed.org/publications/the-region/lender-of-more-than-last-resort; James Dolley, "The Industrial Advance Program of the Federal Reserve System," The Quarterly Journal of Economics, vol. 50, no. 2, February 1936, p. 229.

[5] Nationally chartered banks are required to be members of the Federal Reserve System. State chartered banks have the option of becoming members. Until the Monetary Control Act of 1980 (P.L. 96-221), only member banks were allowed to borrow at the discount window.

[6] For more information, see CRS Report R42150, Systemically Important or "Too Big to Fail" Financial Institutions, by Marc Labonte.

[7] Total does not include asset guarantees for Citigroup and Bank of America, under which funds were never used.

[8] One facility, Maiden Lane I, still held more than $1 billion of assets at the end of 2014. It has no debt and is not authorized to purchase additional assets.

[9] In addition to the $30 billion in net income received by the Fed, Treasury received an additional $17.6 billion as net income on the sale of equity that the Fed originally received (and subsequently transferred to the Treasury) as recompense for the Fed's loan to AIG.

[10] Profits are defined here as payments received in excess of principal outlayed. It does not net out administrative expenses, which are not reported separately for each facility. This report

does not consider whether the Fed earned economic profits on these transactions. For example, the income from these transactions may have been partially offset by lost income if the Fed offset those facilities by holding fewer Treasury securities on its balance sheet. One study attempts to estimate this effect for the Fed's broadly based facilities (but not for its special assistance to firms deemed "too big to fail.") For Section 13(3) facilities, it estimates that the facilities earned $8.1 billion in interest and fee income, but the "cost of funds" for those programs was $1.1 billion, so the Fed earned $7 billion net income over the life of the programs. See Michael Fleming and Nicholas Klagge, "Income Effects of Federal Reserve Liquidity Facilities," Federal Reserve Bank of New York, Current Issues in Economics and Finance, vol. 17, no. 1, 2011, http://www.nyfedeconomists.org/research/current_issues/ci17-1.pdf.

[11] Under a non-recourse loan, the creditor has no right to seek payment beyond the collateral posted in the event that the loan is not repaid.

[12] For more information, see Federal Reserve, Office of the Inspector General, The Federal Reserve's Section 13(3) Lending Facilities to Support Overall Market Liquidity, November 2010, http://oig.federalreserve.gov/reports/FRS_Lending_Facilities_Report_final-11-23-10_web.pdf. See also U.S. Government Accountability Office (GAO), Federal Reserve System: Opportunities Exist to Strengthen Policies and Processes for Managing Emergency Assistance, GAO-11-696, July 21, 2011, http://www.gao.gov/new.items/d11696.pdf. The Fed was required to report to Congress on assistance provided pursuant to Section 13(3); these reports are posted at http://www.federalreserve.gov/ monetarypolicy/bst_reports.htm. See also the Fed's website Credit and Liquidity Programs and the Balance Sheet, available at http://www.federalreserve.gov/monetarypolicy/bst_archive.htm.

[13] Other Federal Reserve and federal emergency programs beyond the scope of this report were aimed at supporting mortgage-backed securities (MBS).

[14] For more information, see CRS Report R43345, Shadow Banking: Background and Policy Issues, by Edward V. Murphy.

[15] U.S. Government Accountability Office, Federal Reserve System: Opportunities Exist to Strengthen Policies and Processes for Managing Emergency Assistance, GAO-11-696, July 21, 2011, Tables 12, 20, 25, 27, 31, http://www.gao.gov/new.items/d11696.pdf.

[16] For more information, see CRS Report R42150, Systemically Important or "Too Big to Fail" Financial Institutions, by Marc Labonte.

[17] As described in the reports pursuant to Section 129, available at http://www .federalreserve.gov/monetarypolicy/bst_reports.htm. In the case of Bank of America, losses were greatest at Merrill Lynch, which Bank of America was in the process of acquiring. The Fed (and Treasury) may have been most concerned that if Bank of America was not offered special assistance, the merger would fall through and Merrill Lynch would experience a disorderly failure.

[18] The solvency of Bear Stearns and AIG is analyzed in William Cline and Joseph Gagnon, Lehman Died, Bagehot Lives: Why Did the Fed and Treasury Let a Major Wall Street Bank Fail?, Peterson Institute for International Economics, Policy Brief no. PB 13-21, http://www.piie.com/publications/pb/pb13-21.pdf.

[19] "JPMorgan Took a Bath on Bear Stearns Sale: Dimon," Reuters, October 10, 2012, http://www.cnbc.com/id/ 49361397/.

[20] Chairman Ben S. Bernanke, Remarks before the Committee on Banking, Housing, and Urban Affairs, U.S. Senate September 23, 2008, available at http://www.federalreserve.gov/newsevents/testimony/bernanke20080923a1.htm.

[21] For more information on the discount window, see https://www.frbdiscountwindow.org/en/Pages/GeneralInformation/The-Discount-Window.aspx.

[22] The interpretation of the statute that follows each bullet is based on Alexander Mehra, "Legal Authority in Unusual and Exigent Circumstances: The Federal Reserve and the Financial Crisis," University Of Pennsylvania Journal of Business Law, vol. 13, no. 1, pp. 221-227.

[23] Unusual and exigent circumstances is not defined, but is considered a high threshold. See Alexander Mehra, "Legal Authority in Unusual and Exigent Circumstances: The Federal Reserve and the Financial Crisis," University Of Pennsylvania Journal of Business Law, vol. 13, no. 1, pp. 221-227, citing Thomas C. Baxter, Jr., general counsel, Fed. Reserve Bank of N.Y., "The Legal Position of the Central Bank, The Case of the Federal Reserve Bank of New York," January 19, 2009, available at https://www.google.com/search?q=thomas+c.+Baxter%2C+Jr.%2C+The+Legal+Position+of+the+Central+bank&ie=utf-8&oe=utf-8.

[24] jf five governors are not available, the decision can be made unanimously by the governors available (12 U.S.C. 248r). On at least one occasion in 2008, because of vacancies on the Federal Reserve Board action under Section 13(3) was approved with only four governors voting. See Federal Reserve, Report Pursuant to Section 129: Bridge Loan to The Bear Stearns Companies, http://www.federalreserve.gov/monetarypolicy/files/129bearstearns bridgeloan.pdf; Federal Open Market Committee, Conference Call of the Federal Open Market Committee on March 10, 2008, http://www.federalreserve.gov/monetarypolicy/files/FOMC20080310confcall.pdf.

[25] According to a working paper by legal counsel at the Fed, this requirement placed "virtually no restrictions on the form a written credit instrument must take in order to be eligible for discount." David H. Small and James A. Clouse, "The Scope of Monetary Policy Actions Authorized under the Federal Reserve Act," Federal Reserve, working paper, July 19, 2004, p. 15.

[26] The discount window standards referenced here state that rates shall be "fixed with a view of accommodating commerce and business" (12 U.S.C. 357).

[27] Alexander Mehra, "Legal Authority in Unusual and Exigent Circumstances: The Federal Reserve and the Financial Crisis," University Of Pennsylvania Journal of Business Law, vol. 13, no. 1, p. 235. This article also presents arguments that the Fed nevertheless exceeded its legal authority for some transactions under Section 13(3).

[28] The Commercial Paper Funding Facility (CPFF) was also structured as a limited liability corporation (LLC) that purchased commercial paper and was financed by loans from the Fed. The Fed also created LLCs associated with the Term Asset-Backed Securities Loan Facility (TALF).

[29] Board of Governors of the Federal Reserve System, Report Pursuant to Section 129: Authorization to Provide Residual Financing to Bank of America Corporation, January 15, 2009, http://www.federalreserve.gov/monetarypolicy/files/129bofa.pdf.

[30] Federal Reserve, Report Pursuant to Section 129: Secured Credit Facility Authorized for American International Group, September 16, 2008, http //www.federalreserve.gov/monetarypolicy/files/129aigseccreditfacility.pdf.

[31] Senator Christopher Dodd, Congressional Record, November 27, 1991, p. 36131. See also Walker Todd, "FDICIA's Emergency Liquidity Provisions," Federal Reserve Bank of Cleveland, Economic Review, Third Quarter, 1993.

[32] See, for example, the Joint Explanatory Statement of the Committee of the Conference to P.L. 111-203, H.Rept. 111- 517, 111th Congress, June 29, 2010.

[33] The Dodd-Frank Act left three requirements in the original statute largely unchanged: (1) a finding of unusual and exigent circumstances; (2) that interest rates be set consistent with statute governing the discount window; and (3) a finding that the borrower be unable to access private credit.

[34] See, for example, Chairman Ben S. Bernanke, "Federal Reserve Programs To Strengthen Credit Markets And The Economy," Testimony Before the Committee on Financial Services, U.S. House of Representatives, February 10, 2009, http://www.federalreserve.gov/newsevents/testimony/bernanke20090210a.htm.

[35] For more information, see the FDIC website https://www.fdic.gov/resauthority/.

[36] Ben Bernanke, "Warren-Vitter and the Lender of Last Resort," Brookings Institution, blog, May 15, 2015, http://www.brookings.edu/blogs/ben-bernanke/posts/2015/05/15-warren-vitter-proposal.

[37] Federal Reserve, "Federal Reserve Board Seeks Comment on Proposed Amendments to Regulation A Regarding Emergency Lending Authority," press release, December 23, 2013, http://www.federalreserve.gov/newsevents/press/bcreg/20131223a.htm. For more information, see CRS Legal Sidebar WSLG1247, Fed's Emergency Lending Rule Not Finalized A Year After Public Comment Period, by M. Maureen Murphy.

[38] Comment letters are posted on the Fed's website at http://www.federalreserve.gov/apps/foia/ViewComments.aspx? doc_id=R-1476&doc_ver=1.

[39] This debate is discussed below in the section entitled "How Much Discretion Should the Fed Be Granted?"

[40] Federal Reserve, "Extensions of Credit by Federal Reserve Banks," 80 Federal Register 78959, December 18, 2015, available at https://www.gpo.gov/fdsys/pkg/FR-2015-12-18/pdf/2015-30584.pdf.

[41] These reports are available at http://www.federalreserve.gov/monetarypolicy/bst_reports.htm.

[42] The records can be accessed at http://www.federalreserve.gov/newsevents/reform_transaction.htm.

[43] The audit is available at U.S. Government Accountability Office, Federal Reserve System: Opportunities Exist to Strengthen Policies and Processes for Managing Emergency Assistance, GAO-11-696, July 21, 2011, http://www.gao.gov/new.items/d11696.pdf.

[44] For more information on critical functions, see Financial Stability Oversight Council, "Authority to Require Supervision and Regulation of Certain Nonbank Financial Companies," 77 Federal Register 21657, April 11, 2012, http://www.treasury.gov/initiatives/fsoc/rulemaking/Documents/Authority%20to%20Require%20Supervision%20and%20Regulation%20of%20Certain%20Nonbank%20Financial%20 Companies.pdf.

[45] Another question raised by the crisis is whether foreign firms should have access to the Fed's broadly based emergency facilities. For each facility, foreign firms were not eligible to participate, but U.S. affiliates of foreign firms or foreign affiliates of U.S. firms were, depending on the facility. Firms with foreign parent companies were large users of some facilities. For example, 59% of credit extended under the CPFF went to U.S. subsidiaries of foreign firms. Source: U.S. Government Accountability Office, Federal Reserve System: Opportunities Exist to Strengthen Policies and Processes for Managing Emergency Assistance, GAO-11-696, July 21, 2011, http://www.gao.gov/new.items/d11696.pdf, Figure 10.

[46] Firms enter a code of conduct agreement upon registering with the Fed as primary dealers, but the Fed does not regulate them for safety and soundness in their capacity as primary dealers. In the words of the New York Fed, "the nature of its relationship with primary dealers is a

counterparty relationship, not a regulatory one." Federal Reserve Bank of New York, Administration of Relationships with Primary Dealers, January 2010, https://www.newyorkfed.org/markets/pridealers_policies.html.

[47] The Fed bought some commercial paper issued by nonfinancial firms through the CPFF. Because commercial paper has short maturities, this action can be characterized as providing liquidity rather than long-term credit.

[48] Direct lending to the federal government is prohibited by Section 14 of the Federal Reserve Act.

[49] The Fed is allowed to purchase a narrow range of securities under Section 14 of the Federal Reserve Act. Few securities issued by private firms are permitted besides bank acceptances and bills of exchange, subject to limitations. The Fed has purchased neither in modern times. For more information, see David H. Small and James A. Clouse, "The Scope of Monetary Policy Actions Authorized under the Federal Reserve Act," Federal Reserve, working paper, July 19, 2004, Section 3.4.

[50] For more information, see CRS Legal Sidebar WSLG1300, Court Finds AIG's Bail-Out Terms Constitute an Illegal Exaction but Awards No Damages, by M. Maureen Murphy and David H. Carpenter.

[51] Chairman Jeb Hensarling, comment letter to the Federal Reserve, docket number R-1476, January 13, 2014.

[52] Ben Bernanke, "Warren-Vitter and the Lender of Last Resort," Brookings Institution, blog, May 15, 2015, http://www.brookings.edu/blogs/ben-bernanke/posts/2015/05/15-warren-vitter-proposal.

[53] According to the legal counsel of the NY Fed, "The Congress that enacted Section 13(3) in the 1930's envisioned the Federal Reserve lending to companies, but it surely did not envision the Fed lending to an LLC, because that legal form of organization would not be invented for another 40 years." Thomas Baxter, "The Legal Position of the Central Bank. The Case of the Federal Reserve Bank of New York," speech delivered to Regulatory Response to the Financial Crisis conference, January 19, 2009.

[54] This report takes no position on whether the Fed should bail out failing firms. Bailing out firms poses tradeoffs between potential benefits to financial stability in the short run and potential costs, including moral hazard and risks to taxpayers.

[55] For details on third-party vendors, see Federal Reserve, Office of the Inspector General, The Federal Reserve's Section 13(3) Lending Facilities to Support Overall Market Liquidity, November 2010, p. 25 http://oig.federalreserve.gov/reports/ FRS_Lending_Facilities_Report_final-11-23-10_web.pdf. The New York Fed's contracts with third-party vendors are posted at http://www.newyorkfed.org/aboutthefed/vendor_information.html.

[56] Governor Jerome H. Powell, "'Audit the Fed' and Other Proposals," speech at the Catholic University of America, Columbus School of Law, Washington, DC, February 9, 2015, http://www.federalreserve.gov/newsevents/speech/ powell20150209a.htm.

[57] Chair Janet Yellen, Letter to Honorable Paul Ryan and Honorable Nancy Pelosi, November 16, 2015, http://www.federalreserve.gov/foia/files/ryan-pelosi-letter-20151116.pdf.

[58] Chairman Jeb Hensarling, "Reining in a Sprawling Federal Reserve," Wall Street Journal, November 19, 2015, http://www.wsj.com/articles/reining-in-a-sprawling-federal-reserve-1447978230?alg=y.

[59] In an earlier provision of the Dodd-Frank Act that was not enacted, total assistance under Section 13(3) would have been limited to $4 trillion.

60 Walter Bagehot, Lombard Street: A Description of the Money Market (New York: Charles Scribner's Sons, 1873).

[61] The reliability of market benchmarks is another issue. In some cases, the rate charged by the Fed was tied to LIBOR, and several banks have settled legal cases related to the manipulation of LIBOR during the financial crisis.

[62] Gary Gorton and Andrew Metrick, "The Federal Reserve and Panic Prevention," Journal of Economic Perspectives, vol. 27, no. 4, Fall 2013, p. 53.

[63] James Butkiewicz, "The Reconstruction Finance Corporation, the Gold Standard, and the Banking Panic of 1933," Southern Economic Journal, vol. 66, no. 2, October 1999, p. 271.

[64] Another option for addressing these types of questions would be to allow GAO, the Fed's Inspector General, or some other outside group to investigate confidential material without releasing it to the public.

[65] For more information, see New York Fed documents collection on the TSLF posted at http://www.newyorkfed.org/ markets/tslf.html.

[66] The official list of current primary dealers is posted at http://www.newyorkfed.org/ markets/pridealers_current.html. Lists of past primary dealers are available at http://www.newyorkfed.org/markets/Dealer_Lists_1960_to_2014.xls.

[67] For more information, see New York Fed documents collection on the PDCF posted at http://www.newyorkfed.org/ markets/pdcf.html; Tobias Adrian et al., The Federal Reserve's Primary Dealer Credit Facility, Current Issues in Economics and Finance, vol. 15, no. 4, August 2009, http://www.newyorkfed.org/research/current_issues/ci15-4.pdf.

[68] Figure cited in Fed Chairman Ben Bernanke, "Financial Reform to Address Systemic Risk," speech at the Council on Foreign Relations, March 10, 2009, http://www.federal reserve.gov/newsevents/speech/bernanke20090310a.htm.

[69] For more information, see New York Fed documents collection on the CPFF posted at http://www.newyorkfed.org/ markets/cpff.html; Tobias Adrian et al., "The Federal Reserve's Commercial Paper Funding Facility," Federal Reserve Bank of New York, Economic Policy Review, May 2011, p. 25, http://www.newyorkfed.org/research/ epr/11v17n1/ 1105adri.pdf.

[70] U.S. Government Accountability Office (GAO), Federal Reserve System: Opportunities Exist to Strengthen Policies and Processes for Managing Emergency Assistance, GAO-11-696, July 21, 2011, Table 12, http://www.gao.gov/ new.items/d11696.pdf.

[71] To comply with statute, the CPFF was set up as a special purpose vehicle (SPV) controlled by the Fed that borrowed from the Fed to finance its commercial paper purchases.

[72] For more information, see New York Fed documents collection on TALF posted at http://www.newyorkfed.org/ markets/talf.html and http://www.newyorkfed. org/research/ epr/12v18n3/1210ashc.pdf; Sumit Agarwal, Jacqueline Barrett, Crystal Cun, and Mariacristina De Nardi, "The asset-backed securities markets, the crisis, and TALF," Federal Reserve Bank of Chicago, Economic Perspectives, 4Q/2010, p. 101, https://www.chicagofed.org/~/media/publications/economic-perspectives/2010/4qtr2010-part1-agarwal-barrett-cun-denardi-pdf.pdf.

[73] Federal Reserve, "Federal Reserve Announces the Creation of the Term Asset-Backed Securities Loan Facility (TALF)," press release, November 25, 2008.

[74] On July 20, 2010, Treasury reduced its loss exposure to $4.3 billion, maintaining the 10% maximum loss exposure in light of the actual loans outstanding when the program ended.

[75] Federal Reserve, Final Report Pursuant to Section 129(b), November 21, 2014, http://www.federalreserve.gov/ monetarypolicy/files/129periodicupdate20141121.pdf.

[76] For more information, see CRS Report R42150, Systemically Important or "Too Big to Fail" Financial Institutions, by Marc Labonte.

[77] Federal Reserve Bank of New York, Maiden Lane Transactions, http://www.newyorkfed.org/markets/ maidenlane.html.

[78] For details on the Fed's assistance, see New York Fed, Actions Related to AIG, http://www.newyorkfed.org/ aboutthefed/aig/index.html. For more information on the federal assistance to AIG, see CRS Report R42953, Government Assistance for AIG: Summary and Cost, by Baird Webel.

[79] See, for example, "U.S. to Take Over AIG in $85 Billion Bailout; Central Banks Inject Cash as Credit Dries Up," Wall Street Journal, September 17, 2008, pp. A1-A6.

[80] In October 2008, AIG also announced that it had applied to the Fed's broadly available Commercial Paper Funding Facility (CPFF) and was approved to borrow up to $20.9 billion at the facility's standard terms. At its peak use in January 2009, AIG had commercial paper worth $16.1 billion outstanding from the CPFF. AIG continued to access the facility until it expired in February 2010. Over the life of the facility, AIG paid $0.4 billion in interest to the CPFF. AIG's use of the CPFF is included in the CPFF totals, not the AIG totals, in this report.

[81] AIG issued $1.6 billion of additional preferred shares to the government in recognition of accrued, unpaid dividends on the initial $40 billion in assistance.

[82] U.S. Treasury, "Joint Statement by Treasury, Federal Reserve, and FDIC on Citigroup," press release hp-1287, November 23, 2008.

[83] For information on Citigroup's TARP shares, see CRS Report R41427, Troubled Asset Relief Program (TARP): Implementation and Status, by Baird Webel.

[84] U.S. Treasury, "Treasury Prices Sale of Citigroup Subordinated Notes for Proceeds of $894 Million, Providing an Additional Profit for Taxpayers on TARP Citigroup Investment," press release, February 5, 2013, http://www.treasury.gov/press-center/press-releases/ Pages/tg1841.aspx; U.S. Treasury, "Taxpayers Receive $10.5 Billion In Proceeds Today From Final Sale Of Treasury Department Citigroup Common Stock," press release, December 10, 2010, http://www.financialstability.gov/latest/pr_12102010.html; Federal Reserve, "Support for Specific Institutions," available at http://www.federalreserve.gov/ monetarypolicy/bst_supportspecific.htm.

[85] U.S. Treasury, "Treasury, Federal Reserve, and the FDIC Provide Assistance to Bank of America," press release hp1356, January 15, 2009.

[86] U.S. Treasury, "Asset Guarantee Program," available at http://www.treasury.gov/initiatives/financial-stability/TARPPrograms/bank-investment-programs /agp/Pages/overview.aspx The termination agreement is available at http://www.treasury.gov/initiatives/financial-stability/programs/investment-programs/agp/ Documents/BofA%20-%20Termination%20Agreement%20-%20executed.pdf.

In: Emergency Lending ...
Editor: Felicia Estrada

ISBN: 978-1-63485-393-4

Chapter 2

GOVERNMENT ASSISTANCE FOR AIG: SUMMARY AND COST*

Baird Webel

SUMMARY

American International Group (AIG), one of the world's major insurers, was the largest direct recipient of government financial assistance during the recent financial crisis. At the maximum, the Federal Reserve (Fed) and the Treasury committed approximately $182.3 billion in specific extraordinary assistance for AIG and another $15.9 billion through a more widely available lending facility. The amount actually disbursed to assist AIG reached a maximum of $184.6 billion in April 2009. In return, AIG paid interest and dividends on the funding and the U.S. Treasury ultimately received a 92% ownership share in the company. As of December 14, 2012, the government assistance for AIG ended. All Federal Reserve loans have been repaid and the Treasury has sold all of the common equity that resulted from the assistance.

Going into the financial crisis, the overarching AIG holding company was regulated by the Office of Thrift Supervision (OTS), but most of its U.S. operating subsidiaries were regulated by various states. Because AIG was primarily an insurer, it was largely outside of the normal Federal Reserve facilities that lend to thrifts facing liquidity

* This is an edited, reformatted and augmented version of a Congressional Research Service publication R42953, prepared for Members and Committees of Congress, dated August 14, 2013.

difficulties and it was also outside of the normal Federal Deposit Insurance Corporation (FDIC) receivership provisions that apply to banking institutions. September 2008 saw a panic in financial markets marked by the failure of large financial institutions, such as Fannie Mae, Freddie Mac, and Lehman Brothers. In addition to suffering from the general market downturn, AIG faced extraordinary losses resulting largely from two sources: (1) the AIG Financial Products subsidiary, which specialized in financial derivatives and was primarily the regulatory responsibility of the OTS; and (2) a securities lending program, which used securities originating in the state-regulated insurance subsidiaries. In the panic conditions prevailing at the time, the Federal Reserve determined that "a disorderly failure of AIG could add to already significant levels of financial market fragility" and stepped in to support the company. Had AIG not been given assistance by the government, bankruptcy seemed a near certainty. The Federal Reserve support was later supplemented and ultimately replaced by assistance from the U.S. Treasury's Troubled Asset Relief Program (TARP).

The AIG rescue produced unexpected financial returns for the government. The Fed loans were completely repaid and it directly received $18.1 billion in interest, dividends, and capital gains. In addition, another $17.5 billion in capital gains from the Fed assistance accrued to the Treasury. The $67.8 billion in TARP assistance, however, resulted in a negative return to the government, as only $54.4 billion was recouped from asset sales and $0.9 billion was received in dividend payments. If one offsets the negative return to TARP of $12.5 billion with the $35.6 billion in positive returns for the Fed assistance, the entire assistance for AIG showed a positive return of approximately $23.1 billion. It should be noted that these figures are the simple cash returns from the AIG transactions and do not take into account the full economic costs of the assistance. Fully accounting for these costs would result in lower returns to the government, although no agency has performed such a full assessment of the AIG assistance. The latest Congressional Budget Office (CBO) estimate of the budgetary cost of the TARP assistance for AIG, which is a broader economic analysis of the cost, found a loss of $15 billion compared with the $12.5 billion cash loss. CBO does not, however, regularly perform cost estimates on Federal Reserve actions.

Congressional interest in the AIG intervention relates to oversight of the Federal Reserve and TARP, as well as general policy measures to promote financial stability. Specific attention has focused on perceived corporate profligacy, particularly compensation for AIG employees, which was the subject of a hearing in the 113th Congress and legislation in the 111th Congress.

INTRODUCTION

In 2007, American International Group (AIG) was the fifth-largest insurer in the world with $110 billion in overall revenues. In the United States, it ranked second in property/casualty insurance premiums ($37.7 billion/7.5% market share) and first in life insurance premiums ($53.0 billion/8.9%). For particular lines, AIG ranked first in surplus lines, ninth in private passenger auto, first in overall commercial lines (fifth in commercial auto), and fourth in mortgage guaranty. It was outside the top 10 in homeowners insurance.[1] According to the National Association of Insurance Commissioners (NAIC), AIG had more than 70 state-regulated insurance subsidiaries in the United States, with more than 175 non-insurance or foreign entities under the general holding company.

Although primarily operating as an insurer, prior to the crisis AIG was overseen at the holding company level by the federal Office of Thrift Supervision (OTS) because the company owned a relatively small thrift subsidiary. The bulk of the company's insurance operations were regulated by the individual state regulators as, per the 1945 McCarran-Ferguson Act,[2] the states act as the primary regulators of the business of insurance. Because AIG was primarily an insurer, it was largely outside of the normal Federal Reserve (Fed) facilities that lend to thrifts (and banks) facing liquidity difficulties and it was also outside of the normal Federal Deposit Insurance Corporation (FDIC) receivership provisions that apply to FDIC-insured depository institutions.

AIG, as did most financial institutions, suffered losses on a wide variety of financial instruments in 2008. The exceptional losses which resulted in the essential failure of AIG arose primarily from two sources: the derivative activities of the AIG Financial Products (AIGFP) subsidiary and the securities lending activities managed by AIG Investments with securities largely from the AIG insurance subsidiaries. Regulatory oversight of these sources was split. The OTS was responsible for oversight of AIGFP, while the state insurance regulators were responsible for oversight of the insurance subsidiaries which supplied the securities lending operations, and would ultimately bear losses if the securities, or their equivalent value, could not be returned.

With the company facing losses on various operations, AIG experienced a significant decline in its stock price and downgrades from the major credit rating agencies in 2008.[3] These downgrades led to immediate demands for significant amounts of collateral (approximately $14 billion to $15 billion in collateral payments, according to contemporary press reports).[4] As financial demands on the company mounted, bankruptcy appeared a possibility, as occurred with Lehman Brothers in the same timeframe. Fears about the spillover effects from such a failure brought calls for government action to avert such a failure. Many feared that AIG was "too big to fail"[5] due to the potential for widespread disruption to financial markets resulting from such a failure. AIG's size was not the only concern in this regard, but also its innumerable connections to other financial institutions.

The New York Insurance Superintendent, primary regulator of many of the AIG insurance subsidiaries, led an effort to provide the parent AIG holding company with access to up to $20 billion in cash from AIG's insurance subsidiaries, which were perceived as solvent and relatively liquid. Ultimately, this transfer did not take place and efforts to find private funding for AIG failed as well; instead, the Federal Reserve approved an extraordinary loan of up to $85 billion in September 2008. As AIG's financial position weakened following the initial Fed loan, several rounds of additional funding were provided to AIG by both the Fed and the Treasury's Troubled Asset Relief Program (TARP). Assistance to AIG was restructured several times, including loosening of the terms of the assistance[6] (see *Appendix A* below for more complete discussion of the changes to AIG's assistance).

The 2010 Dodd-Frank Act[7] overhauled the financial regulatory structure in the United States. Of particular note with regard to AIG, the act moved all federal financial holding company regulation to the Federal Reserve and moved the oversight of thrift subsidiaries to the Office of the Comptroller of the Currency. Thus, both the AIG holding company and the AIG thrift subsidiary are currently overseen by different agencies than before the crisis.[8] In addition, the act created a Financial Stability Oversight Council (FSOC) and the possibility of enhanced regulation by the Fed of institutions deemed systemically important. AIG was designated as systemically significant in July 2013, and will thus be subject to Fed oversight going forward.[9] The act also put restrictions on the Federal Reserve's lending authority that would limit its ability to make future extraordinary assistance available to individual companies, as was done in the case of AIG. The Dodd-Frank Act did not create a federal insurance regulator; thus the states continue to be the primary regulators of the various insurance operations of AIG.

The assistance for AIG has provoked controversy on several different levels. Significant attention, and anger, has been directed at questions of employee compensation. Following reports of bonuses being paid for employees of AIGFP, the House passed legislation (H.R. 1664, 111th Congress) aimed at prohibiting "unreasonable and excessive compensation and compensation not based on performance standards" for TARP recipients, including AIG (see *Appendix B* for additional information on executive compensation restrictions under TARP). Issues around TARP compensation continue in the 113th Congress, with the House Committee on Oversight & Government Reform's Subcommittee on Economic Growth, Job Creation & Regulatory Affairs holding a hearing entitled "Bailout Rewards: The Treasury Department's Continued Approval of Excessive Pay for Executives at Taxpayer-Funded Companies" on February 26, 2013.[10]

Questions have also been raised about the transparency and legality of the assistance. Although the billions of dollars in government assistance went to the AIG, in many cases, it can be argued that AIG has acted as an intermediary for this assistance. In short order after drawing on government assistance, substantial funds flowed out of AIG to entities on the other side of AIG's financial transactions, such as securities lending or credit default swaps. Seen from this view, the true beneficiary of many of the federal funds that flowed to AIG was not AIG itself, but instead AIG's counterparties, who may not have received full payment in the event of a bankruptcy. In the interest of transparency, many argued that AIG's counterparties, particularly those who received payments facilitated by government assistance, should be identified. Many of these counterparties were only identified after public and congressional pressure.[11]

Lawsuits challenging the legality of the government actions relating to the assistance, particularly the equity taken as part of this assistance, have been filed by Starr International Company, Inc. (Starr). This company is owned by Maurice "Hank" Greenberg, formerly the CEO of AIG and a major stockholder in the company. Starr has sought compensation for the allegedly unconstitutional taking of AIG shareholder property without compensation in connection with the federal assistance package rescuing AIG from bankruptcy. The Board of Directors of AIG declined to join this suit in January 2013, but it is still pending before the Court of Federal Claims.[12]

SUMMARY OF GOVERNMENT ASSISTANCE TO AIG

The extraordinary direct government assistance for AIG that began in September 2008 has ended. All loans to assist AIG have been repaid and the assets purchased from AIG by Federal Reserve entities have been sold. The common equity holdings in AIG that resulted from both Federal Reserve and U.S. Treasury TARP assistance for AIG have been sold. The final connection between the government and AIG was a relatively small amount of warrants issued to the Treasury as part of the TARP assistance. AIG repurchased these warrants for approximately $25 million on March 1, 2013.[13] With the sale of the TARP equity, the TARP corporate governance and executive compensation restrictions imposed on AIG were lifted.

The government assistance for AIG took a variety of different forms, with the initial Federal Reserve loans followed by TARP assistance in three major restructurings in November 2008, March 2009, and September 2010. The following briefly summarizes the primary types of assistance (see *Appendix A* for more complete details).

Federal Reserve Loans to AIG

The initial assistance for AIG came in the form of an $85 billion loan commitment announced on September 16, 2008. In addition to a high, variable interest rate,[14] the government received a nearly 80% share of the common equity in AIG. This loan was augmented by an additional $37.8 billion loan commitment in October 2008, which was collateralized by securities from the AIG securities lending program. The maximum amount outstanding under these loans was over $90 billion in October 2008. The limit on the Fed loan was reduced to $60 billion in November 2008 and $35 billion in March 2009. The 2009 reduction occurred as the Fed accepted $25 billion in AIG subsidiary equity as partial repayment of the loans. The loans were eventually repaid in January 2011, primarily through cash gained by AIG from sales of various assets and from TARP assistance. The Fed received a total of $8.2 billion in interest and dividends from these loans and the common equity stake resulting from the loans was sold by the Treasury for $17.5 billion. Federal Reserve profits are mostly remitted to the Treasury and such remittances more than doubled from 2007 to 2010.[15]

Federal Reserve Loans to Finance Asset Purchases from AIG

In November 2008, the Fed loan to AIG was partially replaced by Fed loans to Limited Liability Corporations (LLCs) created and controlled by the Fed, which were known as Maiden Lane II and Maiden Lane III.[16] Up to $52.5 billion in loans from the Fed were committed to Maiden Lanes II and III with $43.8 billion actually disbursed.[17] These LLCs purchased various securities, which were an ongoing financial drain on AIG at the time. After purchase, these securities were held by the LLCs and then sold as market conditions improved. All the loans were repaid by June 2012, and the facilities ultimately returned an additional $9.5 billion in interest and other gains to the Fed.

AIG Commercial Paper Funding Facility Borrowing

The Commercial Paper Funding Facility (CPFF) was created by the Federal Reserve in 2008 as a widely available vehicle to provide liquidity during the financial crisis.[18] AIG and its subsidiaries were approved to borrow up to a maximum of $20.9 billion, with actual borrowing reaching $16.1 billion in January 2009. AIG's CPFF borrowing is typically not included in the reporting of AIG assistance done by the Fed and Treasury. This borrowing, however, occurred at the same time as AIG was accessing the other Fed loans and TARP assistance and likely was preferred over these sources because CPFF charged lower interest rates[19] and individual CPFF borrowers and borrowing amounts were not reported by the Fed at the time. The Dodd-Frank Act required the Fed to report full details of the CPFF and other Fed facilities.[20] This reporting shows AIG borrowing beginning in October 2008 and extending until April 2010. Although interest amounts were not reported, according to CRS estimates based on the principal amounts and interest rates that were reported, the Fed appears to have received approximately $0.4 billion in interest from AIG's CPFF borrowing.

TARP Assistance for AIG

In November 2008, $40 billion in TARP assistance was committed to AIG, and it was disbursed through Treasury purchase of AIG preferred equity.[21] The commitment was increased to nearly $70 billion in March 2009, and the maximum level of disbursement of $67.8 billion was reached in January 2011, primarily to facilitate the withdrawal of Federal Reserve involvement with AIG.[22] Although TARP assistance took the form of preferred equity purchases, $47.5 billion in AIG preferred equity was converted into common equity, which brought the government ownership stake in AIG to a high of 92% in January 2011. The Treasury began selling the common equity in May 2011 and completed the sales in December 2012. In addition to the equity, the Treasury received a relatively small number of stock warrants through TARP, which it sold back to AIG in March 2013.[23] The Treasury received $34.1 billion from its sales of the TARP common equity and approximately $25 million from the warrant sales. AIG completely redeemed the $20.3 billion in unconverted preferred equity in March 2012, and the company paid a total $0.9 billion in cash dividends to the government on this equity. Comparing the total amount disbursed to the total amount recouped shows a $12.5 billion shortfall on the TARP portion of the assistance for AIG.

Table 1 below summarizes the direct government assistance for AIG, including maximum amounts committed by the government, the amounts actually disbursed, and the returns from this assistance.

Indirect Assistance for AIG

Although the loans and preferred equity purchase directly aided AIG, the company also benefited from other actions taken by the U.S. government to address the financial crisis. For example, TARP provided nearly $205 billion in additional capital to U.S. banks in 2008 and early 2009. To the extent that AIG had assets that depended on the health of these banks, or liabilities, such as CDS, that might have increased with the failure of these banks, the TARP assistance for banks would have aided AIG's financial position as well as the financial position of most other financial institutions. If AIG was perceived as being "too big to fail" due to the government assistance, the company may also have received an advantage in insurance markets and in debt markets compared to other firms competing with AIG. The reputational effect of government-backing, however, also had negative effects on the company to the degree that AIG even changed the name of its primary insurance subsidiary. Such second-order effects from the government actions are difficult to quantify and typically are not included in assessments of the assistance for AIG.

Another indirect, but more definite, benefit to AIG from government action during the crisis came from policy rulings by the Internal Revenue Service (IRS).[24] Under normal circumstances, a corporation undergoing a change in control is not able to carry forward previous tax losses.[25] Government holdings gained through TARP, however, generally have not been treated by the IRS as causing such a change in control. AIG was able to report a $17.7 billion accounting gain from these tax benefits in 2011.[26] Economic theory would suggest that these tax benefits resulted in the government receiving a higher price for the AIG shares when they were sold, so the final result may not have been to increase the overall cost of the AIG assistance. Whether or not one includes these tax rulings as specific assistance for AIG, however, would significantly change the assessment of the overall financial results from the assistance. Neither the Treasury nor CBO have included these tax rulings in their assessments of the assistance for AIG.

WHAT DID THE ASSISTANCE FOR AIG COST?

From the above accounting, which largely follows that offered by the Treasury in its announcements,[27] the cost of the AIG assistance seems relatively straightforward. Summing the various amounts of interest, dividends, and equity sales, one arrives at a total of $207.7 billion returned to the Treasury and Federal Reserve compared with a total maximum disbursement of $184.1 billion, for a positive return of $23.1 billion. This cash accounting, however, falls short of a full economic assessment of the assistance for AIG. Such assessments typically include other factors, such as the time value of money (a dollar in 2008 was not worth the same as a dollar in 2012) and the opportunity cost of the funds involved (what would the returns have been if the money involved had been used for other purposes?).

The budgetary cost estimates undertaken by the Congressional Budget Office (CBO) incorporate some broader economic principles in assessing the costs of government actions. In particular, CBO's official budgetary cost estimates for TARP must follow not only the Federal Credit Reform Act,[28] which requires that the present value of the full long-term cost of loans and loan guarantees be recognized, but also that market rates be used in these calculations rather than the lower Treasury borrowing costs.[29] These requirements have the effect of lowering the returns. This effect can be seen by comparing the CBO estimates with the more simple cash accounting above. The latest CBO estimates, which occurred after most of the AIG equity had been sold, saw a budgetary cost of $15 billion attributed to the TARP portion of the AIG assistance,[30] compared to a negative return of $12.5 billion using the simple cash accounting.

The Federal Reserve actions which make up a majority of the returns from the government assistance for AIG are not subject to regular CBO or OMB budgetary cost assessment. CBO did publish a study of the budgetary impact and subsidy cost of the Federal Reserve's response to the financial crisis in May 2010. CBO estimated a cost of $2 billion from the Federal Reserve loans to AIG at their inception,[31] compared to a final positive return of $35.6 billion on a cash accounting basis. The CBO estimates for TARP have become significantly more positive over time, and it is quite possible that, were CBO to redo the estimates at the current date, the estimate for the Federal Reserve actions would become more positive as well.

Table 1. Summary of Direct AIG Assistance

Type of Assistance	Maximum Amount Committed	Maximum Amount Actually Disbursed	Date of Repayment	Gain or Loss (-) on Assistance
Extraordinary Fed Loans to AIG	$122.8 billion (Oct. 2008)	$90.3 billion (Oct. 22, 2008)	Jan. 2011	$25.7 billion
Fed Loans for Asset Purchases	$52.5 billion (Nov. 2008)	$43.8 billion (Dec. 2008)	June 2012	$9.5 billion
Fed Loans through CPFF	$20.9 billion (Nov. 2008)	$16.1 billion (Jan. 2009)	April 2010	$0.4 billion
TARP Preferred Share Purchases	$69.8 billion (March 2009)	$67.8 billion (Jan. 2011)	Dec. 2012	-$12.5 billion
Totals	$198.2 billion (March 2009)	$184.6 billion (April 2009)	Dec. 2012	$23.1 billion

Source: Federal Reserve weekly H.4.1 statistical release; Federal Reserve Board and Federal Reserve Bank of NY data releases; U.S. Treasury TARP Monthly Reports; CRS calculations.

Note: Warrants associated with TARP preferred shares repurchased by AIG in March 2013. The approximately $25 million gain from this is included in the -$12.5 billion loss from the TARP shares.

APPENDIX A. DETAILS OF GOVERNMENT ASSISTANCE FOR AIG

Assistance Prior to TARP Involvement

Initial Loan

On September 16, 2008, the Fed announced, after consultation with the Treasury Department, that it would lend up to $85 billion to AIG over the next two years. Drawing from the loan facility would only occur at the discretion of the Fed. A new CEO was installed after the initial intervention and Fed staff was put on site with the company to oversee operations. The interest rate on the funds drawn from the Fed was 8.5 percentage points above the London Interbank Offered Rate (LIBOR), a rate that banks charge to lend to each other. AIG also was to pay a flat 8.5% interest rate on any funds that it did not draw from the facility. The government received warrants that, if exercised, would give the government a 79.9% ownership stake in AIG. Three independent trustees were to be named by the Fed to oversee the firm for the duration of the loan. The trustees for the AIG Credit Trust were announced on January 16, 2009, and the warrants were later exercised.[32]

This lending facility (and its successors) was secured by the assets of AIG's holding company and non-regulated subsidiaries.[33] In other words, the Fed could seize AIG's assets if AIG failed to honor the terms of the loan. This reduced the risk that the Fed, and the taxpayers, would suffer a loss, assuming, of course, that the Fed would have been willing to seize these assets. The risk still remained that if AIG turned out to be insolvent, its assets might be insufficient to cover the amount it had borrowed from the Fed.

On September 18, 2008, the Fed announced that it had initially lent $28 billion of the $85 billion possible. This amount grew to approximately $61 billion on November 5, 2008, shortly before the restructuring of the loan discussed below in "Federal Reserve Loan Restructuring."[34]

Securities Borrowing Facility[35]

On October 8, 2008, the Fed announced that it was expanding its assistance to AIG by swapping cash for up to $37.8 billion of AIG's investment-grade, fixed-income securities. These securities stemmed from the AIG securities lending program. As some counterparties stopped participating in the lending program, AIG was forced to incur losses on its securities lending investments.[36] AIG needed liquidity from the Fed to cover these losses and counterparty withdrawals. This lending facility was to extend for nearly two years, until September 16, 2010, and advances from the securities borrowing facility to AIG paid an interest rate of 1% over the average overnight repo rate.[37] As of November 5, 2008, shortly before the facility was restructured, $19.9 billion of the $37.8 billion was outstanding.

Although this assistance resembled a typical collateralized loan (the lender receives assets as collateral, and the borrower receives cash), the Fed characterized the agreement as a loan of securities from AIG to the Fed in exchange for cash collateral. The arrangement may have been structured this way due to New York state insurance law provisions regarding insurers using securities as collateral in a loan.[38]

Commercial Paper Funding Facility

The Commercial Paper Funding Facility (CPFF) was initially announced by the Fed on October 7, 2008, as a measure to restore liquidity in the commercial paper market.[39] It was a general facility, open to many recipients, not only AIG. Through the CPFF, the Fed purchased both asset-backed and unsecured commercial paper. Rather than charging an interest rate, the Fed purchased the paper at a discount based on the three-month overnight index swap rate (OIS). Unsecured paper was discounted by 3%, whereas secured paper was discounted by 1%.

AIG announced that, as of November 5, 2008, it had been authorized to issue up to $20.9 billion of commercial paper to the CPFF and had actually issued approximately $15.3 billion of this amount. Subsequent downgrades of AIG's airline leasing subsidiary (ILFC) reduced the maximum amount AIG could access from the CPFF to $15.2 billion in early January 2009. ILFC had approximately $1.7 billion outstanding to the CPFF when it was downgraded; this amount was repaid by January 28, 2009.[40]

On February 17, 2010, the reported total CPFF borrowing outstanding was $2.3 billion.[41] CPFF new purchase of commercial paper expired February 1, 2010, with maximum maturities extending 90 days from this point. Thus, by the end of April 2010, all AIG borrowing from the CPFF was repaid.

Table A-1. Summary of AIG Assistance Before TARP

Program	Maximum Committed Amount of Government Assistance	Government Assistance Outstanding (as Nov. 5, 2008)	Recompense to the Government	Expiration Date
Federal Reserve Loan Federal Reserve Securities Borrowing Facility Commercial Paper Funding Facility	$85 billion $37.8 billion $20.9 billion	$61 billion: (includes principal and interest) $19.9 billion: (includes principal and interest) $15.3 billion	LIBOR+8.5% (drawn amounts); 8.5% (undrawn amounts); 79.9% of AIG equity Overnight repo rate +1% OIS rate+1%; OIS+3%	September 2010 September 2010 February 2010

Source: Federal Reserve EESA Section 129 reports; AIG SEC filings.

November 2008 Revision of Assistance to AIG

On November 10, 2008, the Federal Reserve and the U.S. Treasury announced a restructuring of the federal intervention to support AIG. Following the initial loan, some, notably AIG's former CEO Maurice Greenberg, criticized the terms as overly harsh, arguing that the loan itself might be contributing to AIG's eventual failure as a company. As evidenced by the additional borrowing after the September 16 loan, AIG had continued to see cash flow out of the company.

The revised agreement eased the payment terms for AIG and had three primary parts: (1) restructuring of the initial $85 billion Fed loan, (2) a $40 billion direct capital injection from the Treasury, and (3) up to $52.5 billion in Fed loans used to purchase troubled assets. Separately, AIG continued to access the Fed CPFF as described above.

Federal Reserve Loan Restructuring

The Fed reduced the $85 billion loan facility to $60 billion, extended the time period to five years, and eased the financial terms considerably. Specifically, the interest rate on the amount outstanding was reduced by 5.5 percentage points (to LIBOR plus 3%), and the fee on undrawn funds was reduced by 7.75 percentage points (to 0.75%).

Troubled Asset Relief Program Assistance

Through TARP, the Treasury purchased $40 billion in preferred shares of AIG. In addition to the preferred shares, the Treasury also received warrants for common shares equal to 2% of the outstanding AIG shares. AIG was the first announced non-bank to receive TARP funds. The $40 billion in preferred AIG shares held by the Treasury were slated to pay a 10% dividend per annum, accrued quarterly.[42] The amount of shares held in trust for the benefit of the U.S. Treasury under the previous Fed loan was also reduced so that the total government equity interest in AIG (trust shares plus Treasury warrants) remained under 80% after the TARP intervention.

Purchase of Troubled Assets

Although EESA provided for Treasury purchase of troubled assets under TARP, the troubled asset purchases related to AIG were done by LLCs created and controlled by the Federal Reserve. This structure was similar to that created by the Fed to facilitate the purchase of Bear Stearns by JPMorgan Chase in March 2008. Two LLCs were set up for AIG—Maiden Lane II for residential mortgage-backed securities (RMBS) and Maiden Lane III for collateralized debt obligations (CDO).[43]

Residential Mortgage-Backed Securities/Maiden Lane II

Under the November 2008 restructuring, the RMBS LLC/Maiden Lane II could receive loans up to $22.5 billion by the Fed and $1 billion from AIG to purchase RMBS from AIG's securities lending portfolio. The previous $37.8 billion securities lending loan facility was repaid and terminated following the creation of this LLC. The Fed was credited with interest from its loan to Maiden Lane II at a rate of LIBOR plus 1% for a term of six years, extendable by the Fed. The $1 billion loan from AIG was credited with interest at a rate of LIBOR plus 3%. The AIG loan, however, was subordinate to the Fed's. Any proceeds from Maiden Lane II were to be distributed in the following order: (1) operating expenses of the LLC, (2) principal due to the Fed, (3) interest due to the Fed, and (4) deferred payment and interest due to AIG. Should additional funds remain at the liquidation of the LLC, these remaining funds were to be shared by the Fed and AIG with AIG receiving one-sixth of the value. Ultimately the securities in Maiden Lane II were sufficient to fully repay the loans, with interest. The Fed received approximately $2.3 billion in capital gains, with AIG receiving approximately $460 million.

The actual amount of Fed loan made to Maiden Lane II totaled $19.5 billion of the $22.5 billion maximum. Maiden Lane II purchased RMBS with this amount along with the $1 billion loan from AIG. The securities purchased had a face value of nearly double the purchase price ($39.3 billion).[44]

Collateralized Debt Obligations/Maiden Lane III

Under the November 2008 restructuring, the CDO LLC/Maiden Lane III could receive loans up to $30 billion from the Fed and $5 billion from AIG to purchase CDOs on which AIG had written credit default swaps. At the same time that the CDOs were purchased, the CDS written on these CDOs were terminated, relieving financial pressure on AIG. The Fed and AIG were to be credited with interest from the loans at a rate of LIBOR plus 3% until repaid. The proceeds from Maiden Lane III were to be distributed in the following order: (1) operating expenses of the LLC, (2) principal due to the Fed, (3) interest due to the Fed, and (4) deferred payment and interest due to AIG. Should any funds remain after this distribution, they were to go two-thirds to the Fed and one-third to AIG. Ultimately the securities in Maiden Lane III were sufficient to fully repay the loans, with interest. The Fed received approximately $5.9 billion in capital gains, with AIG receiving approximately $2.9 billion.

The actual amount of the Fed loan to Maiden Lane III was $24.3 billion of the $30 billion maximum, while AIG loaned the LLC $5 billion. In addition to these loans, Maiden Lane III purchase of CDOs was also funded by approximately $35 billion in cash collateral previously posted to holders of CDS by AIGFP. In return for the use of this collateral, AIGFP received approximately $2.5 billion from the LLC. The total par value of CDOs purchased by Maiden Lane III was approximately $62.1 billion.

Table A-2. Summary of AIG Assistance Under November 2008 Plan (amounts as of March 2009)

Program	Maximum Committed Amount of Government Assistance	Government Assistance Outstanding	Recompense to the Government	Expiration Date
TARP Share Purchase	$40 billion	$40 billion (principal); $1.6 billion (dividends)	10% quarterly dividend; warrants for 2% of AIG equity;	Preferred shares outstanding until repurchased.
Federal Reserve Loan	$60 billion	$42.0 billion (includes principal and interest)	3 month LIBOR+3%; 77.9% of AIG equity	September 2013
Commercial Paper Funding Facility	$20.9 billion	$12.2 billion $18.4 billion	OIS rate+1%; OIS+3% 5/6 of equity	October 2009 November 2014
Maiden Lane II	$22.5 billion	(principal); $91 million (interest) $24.0 billion	remaining after loan repayment 2/3 of equity	(loan); assets held until disposed of. November 2014
Maiden Lane III	$30 billion	(principal); $127 million (interest)	remaining after loan repayment	(loan); assets held until disposed of.

Source: Federal Reserve weekly H.1.4 statistical release; Federal Reserve Bank of NY website; U.S. Treasury TARP reports; AIG SEC filings; CRS calculations.

Notes: CPFF and TARP values as of March 31, 2009, other Fed values as of March 25, 2009. The loan amounts to Maiden Lane II and III were from these entities to the Fed, and were not to be repaid by AIG. AIG also had outstanding loans Maiden Lane II and III, which were junior in priority to the Fed loans. The dividends on the TARP share purchase and the interest on the loans were generally allowed to accrue rather than being immediately paid.

A summary of the assistance under the November 2008 plan is presented in *Table A-2.*

March 2009 Revision of Assistance to AIG

On March 2, 2009, the Treasury and Fed announced another revision of the financial assistance to AIG. On the same day, AIG announced a loss of more than $60 billion in the fourth quarter of 2008. In response to the poor results and ongoing financial turmoil, private credit ratings agencies were reportedly considering further downgrading AIG, which would most likely have resulted in further significant cash demands due to collateral calls.[45] According to the Treasury, AIG "continues to face significant challenges, driven by the rapid deterioration in certain financial markets in the last two months of the year and continued turbulence in the markets generally." The revised assistance was intended to "enhance the company's capital and liquidity in order to facilitate the orderly completion of the company's global divestiture program."[46]

The announced revised assistance included the following:

- Exchange of the previous $40 billion in preferred shares purchased through the TARP program for $41.6 billion in preferred shares that more closely resembled common equity, thus improving AIG's financial position. Dividends paid on these new shares remained at 10%, but were non-cumulative and only paid when declared by AIG's Board of Directors. Should dividends not be paid for four consecutive quarters, the government would have had the right to appoint at least two new directors to the board.
- Commitment of up to $29.8 billion[47] in additional preferred share purchases from TARP. Timing of these share purchases was at the discretion of AIG.
- Reduction of interest rate on the existing Fed loan facility by removing the floor of 3.5% over the LIBOR portion of the rate. The rate became three-month LIBOR plus 3%, which was approximately 4.25% at the time.
- Limit on Fed revolving credit facility was reduced from $60 billion to as low as $25 billion.
- Up to $34.5 billion of the approximately $38 billion outstanding on the Fed credit facility was to be repaid by asset transfers from AIG to the

Fed. Specifically, (1) $8.5 billion in ongoing life insurance cash flows were to be securitized by AIG and transferred to the Fed; and (2) approximately $26 billion in equity interests in two of AIG's large foreign life insurance subsidiaries (ALICO and AIA) are to be issued to the Fed. This would effectively transfer a majority stake in these companies to the Fed, but the companies would still be managed by AIG.

A $25 billion repayment of the Fed loan through the transfer of equity interest worth $16 billion in AIA and $9 billion in ALICO was completed on December 1, 2009, with a corresponding reduction in the Fed loan maximum to $35 billion. According to AIG's 2009 annual 10-K filing with the SEC, the repayment through securitization of life insurance cash flows was no longer expected to occur and has not occurred.

Separately, AIG continued to access the Fed's Commercial Paper Funding Facility, which was extended to February 2010.

A summary of assistance under the March 2009 plan is presented in *Table A-3.*

Table A-3. Summary of AIG Assistance Under March 2009 Plan (amounts as of September 2010)

Program	Maximum Committed Amount of Government Assistance	Government Assistance Outstanding	Recompense to the Government	Expiration Date
TARP Share Purchase	$69.8 billion	$47.5 billion (principal); $1.6 billion (dividends)	10% quarterly dividend; warrants for 2% of AIG equity	March 2014; preferred shares outstanding until repurchased
Federal Reserve Loan	$35 billion	$18.9 billion: (includes principal and interest)	3 month LIBOR+3%; 77.9% of AIG equity	September 2013
AIG Subsidiary Equity (accepted as repayment for Fed Loan)	$25 billion	$25 billion (principal); $1 billion (dividends)	5% quarterly dividends	none

Table A-3. (Continued)

Program	Maximum Committed Amount of Government Assistance	Government Assistance Outstanding	Recompense to the Government	Expiration Date
Commercial Paper Funding Facility	$15.9 billion	$0 (facility expired)	OIS rate+1%; OIS+3%	February 2010
Maiden Lane II	$22.5 billion	$13.7 billion (principal); $408 million (interest)	5/6 of equity remaining after loan repayment	November 2014 (loan); assets held until disposed of
Maiden Lane III	$30 billion	$14.6 billion (principal); $499 million (interest)	2/3 of equity remaining after loan repayment	November 2014 (loan); assets held until disposed of

Source: Federal Reserve weekly H.1.4 statistical release; Federal Reserve Bank of NY website; U.S. Treasury TARP reports; AIG SEC filings; CRS calculations.

Notes: Fed amounts as of September 29, 2010; Treasury amounts as of September 30, 2010. The loan amounts to Maiden Lane II and III were from these entities to the Fed, and were not to be repaid by AIG. AIG also has outstanding loans Maiden Lane II and III which were junior in priority to the Fed loans. Quarterly TARP dividends were non-cumulative and paid at AIG's discretion. The dividends on the TARP share purchase and the interest on the loans were generally allowed to accrue rather than being immediately paid.

September 2010 Revision of Assistance for AIG

The structure under which AIG's assistance was ultimately wound down was announced in September 2010 with the multiple transactions involved closing on January 14, 2011. The essence of this restructuring was to (1) end the Fed's direct involvement with AIG through loan repayment and transfer of the Fed's equity interests to the Treasury and (2) convert the government's preferred shares into common shares, which could then be more easily sold. The specific steps included the following:

- Repayment and termination of the Fed loan facility. AIG repaid $19.5 billion to the Fed with cash from the disposal of various assets.

- Transfer to the Treasury of the Fed's preferred equity interests resulting from AIG subsidiaries AIA and Alico. AIG drew $20.3 billion of TARP funds to purchase the Fed's equity in AIG's subsidiaries. This equity was transferred to the Treasury to redeem the TARP funds. The remaining equity (approximately $5.7 billion) was redeemed by funds from sales of other AIG assets. As was the plan when the Fed held the assets, the equity interests held by the Treasury following the transfer were to be redeemed by AIG following further asset sales.
- *Conversion of TARP preferred shares into common equity*. $49.1 billion in TARP preferred share holdings were converted into approximately 1.1 billion common shares worth approximately $43 billion in September 2010.[48] After combining this with the approximately 562.9 million shares (then worth $22 billion) resulting from the initial Fed loan,[49] the Treasury held 1.655 billion shares of AIG common stock, or 92.1% of the AIG common stock.
- *Reduced TARP funding facility*. At AIG's discretion, $2 billion of new Series G preferred shares could be issued by AIG and purchased by the Treasury. These shares would have paid a 5% dividend and any outstanding shares were to convert to common shares at the end of March 2012. None of these shares were issued and this facility was cancelled.
- *Issuance of warrants to private shareholders*. Through an exceptional dividend, AIG issued warrants to existing private shareholders. They extend for 10 years and allow for the purchase of up to 75 million new shares of common stock at the price of $45 a share. These warrants provided a direct benefit to private AIG stockholders while potentially reducing the return on the government's assistance to AIG. This benefit was approximately $1.2 billion at the warrant's initial trading price.[50]

Table 5 summarizes the assistance for AIG after the latest restructuring plan was completed in January 2011, but before any further asset sales or loan repayments.

Table A-4. Summary of AIG Assistance Under Final September 2010 Plan (after closing in mid-January 2011)

			Planned	
Agency	Holdings	Amount	Disposition	Original Source
Treasury	AIG common equity	1.655 billion shares (worth approximately $71.5 billion)	Open market sales	$49.1 billion in TARP preferred shares were converted to 1.1 billion shares; 563 million shares were compensation for Fed loan to AIG (transferred through AIG Credit Trust)
	AIG subsidiary equity	$20.3 billion	Redemption by AIG through equity sales	Fed loan to AIG (transferred using TARP preferred shares)
	AIG preferred shares	$0 (of up to $2 billion)	Redemption by AIG or conversion to common equity	Purchased through TARP
Federal Reserve	Maiden Lane II Maiden Lane III	$12.8 billion (principal); $460 million (interest); $1.4 billion (equity) $12.7 billion (principal); $555 million (interest); $2.6 billion (equity)	Hold to maturity or open market sale Hold to maturity or open market sale	Fed loan to Maiden Lane II Fed loan to Maiden Lane III

Source: Federal Reserve weekly H.4.1 statistical release; Federal Reserve Bank of NY website; U.S. Treasury TARP reports and press releases; AIG SEC filings; CRS calculations.

Note: Values from January 20, 2011.

APPENDIX B. EXECUTIVE COMPENSATION RESTRICTIONS UNDER TARP

By accepting TARP assistance, AIG became subject to the executive compensation standards for their senior executive officers (SEOs, generally the chief executive officer, the chief financial, and the three next most highly compensated officials) generally required under Section 111 of EESA. In addition to these general restrictions, Treasury imposed additional executive compensation restrictions on AIG that are more stringent than for other participants in TARP in recognition of the special assistance received by AIG.[51]

The TARP executive compensation restrictions were amended and strengthened by the 111th Congress in the American Recovery and Reinvestment Act of 2009,[52] which amended Section 111 of EESA to further limit executive compensation for financial institutions receiving assistance under that act. Among other things, for applicable companies, the new language requires the adoption of standards by Treasury that

1. prohibit paying certain executives any bonus, retention, or incentive compensation other than certain long-term restricted stock that has a value not greater than one-third of the total annual compensation of the employee receiving the stock (the determination of how many executives will be subject to these limitations depends on the amount of funds received by the TARP recipient);
2. require the recovery of any bonus, retention award, or incentive compensation paid to SEOs and the next 20 most highly compensated employees based on earnings, revenues, gains or other criteria that are later found to be materially inaccurate;
3. prohibit any compensation plan that would encourage manipulation of the reported earnings of the firm to enhance the compensation of any of its employees;
4. prohibit the provision of "golden parachute" payment to an SEO and the next five most highly compensated employees for departure from a company for any reason, except for payments for services performed or benefits accrued; and
5. prohibit any compensation plan that would encourage manipulation of the reported earnings of the firm to enhance the compensation of any of its employees.

Although Section 111(b)(1) of the amended EESA indicated that these standards applied all TARP recipients until they repay TARP funding, later language (Section 111(b)(3)(iii)) specifically allows bonuses required to be paid under employment contracts executed before February 11, 2009, to go forward notwithstanding the new requirements. The Special Master for TARP Executive Compensation released several specific determinations for AIG compensation.[53]

End Notes

[1] Statistics from The I.I.I. Insurance Fact Book 2009, (New York: Insurance Information Institute, 2009).

[2] P.L. 79-15, 15 U.S.C. §§1011-1015.

[3] In 2005, amid accounting irregularities that ultimately led to the resignation of then-CEO Maurice Greenberg, AIG was downgraded by S&P from AAA to AA+. Further downgrades followed in June 2005 and May 2008. In September 2008, S&P downgraded AIG to A-.

[4] See, for example, "U.S. to Take Over AIG in $85 Billion Bailout; Central Banks Inject Cash as Credit Dries Up," Wall Street Journal, September 17, 2008, pp. A1-A6.

[5] Institutions that are too big to fail are ones that are deemed to be big enough, or interconnected enough, that their failure could create systemic risk, the risk that the financial system as a whole would cease to function smoothly. See CRS Report R40877, Financial Regulatory Reform: Systemic Risk and the Federal Reserve, by Marc Labonte and CRS Report R40417, Macroprudential Oversight: Monitoring Systemic Risk in the Financial System, by Darryl E. Getter for more information on systemic risk and "too big to fail."

[6] The revisions point to a fundamental trade-off between making the terms of the assistance undesirable enough to deter other firms from seeking government assistance and making the terms of assistance so punitive that they exacerbate the financial problems of the recipient firm. It also points to the risk that once a firm has been identified as too big to fail, government assistance to the firm can become open-ended.

[7] P.L. 111-203.

[8] The AIGFP derivatives operation was wound down and largely discontinued. If AIG were to again undertake such an operation, it would fall under the oversight of the Fed.

[9] See http://www.treasury.gov/initiatives/fsoc/designations/ Documents/Basis% 20of%20Final %20Determination%20Regarding%20American%20International%20Group,%20Inc.pdf.

[10] See the committee website at http://oversight.house.gov/hearings/?committees=subcommittee-on-economic-growthjob-creation-and-regulatory-affairs.

[11] For additional detail, please see the section entitled "Who Has Benefited from Assistance to AIG?," in CRS Report R40438, Federal Government Assistance for American International Group (AIG), by Baird Webel, pp. 14-15.

[12] For more information on the Starr lawsuits see CRS Sidebar WSLG271, AIG's Former CEO's $20 Billion Illegal Exaction Claim Based on Federal Reserve's "Illegal" Financial Assistance, by M. Maureen Murphy and CRS Report WSLG366, AIG's Board Will Not Join Shareholder Suits Against Treasury and Federal Reserve, by M. Maureen Murphy.

[13] American International Group, "AIG Repurchases Warrants from U.S. Treasury," press release, March 1, 2013, http://www.aig.com/press-releases_3171_438003.html.

[14] The rate varied between 12% and 12.55% before it was reduced after November 2008.

[15] See CRS Report RL30354, Monetary Policy and the Federal Reserve: Current Policy and Conditions, by Marc Labonte for more information on the Federal Reserve.

[16] A similar LLC, known simply as Maiden Lane, was created to address the failure of the investment bank Bear Stearns in March 2008. The name "Maiden Lane" derives from one of the streets bordering the Federal Reserve Bank of New York headquarters in Manhattan.

[17] AIG also contributed a total of $6 billion to the LLCs and they were structured so that AIG's contribution would bear initial losses, should losses occur. Because of this contribution, AIG shared in the gains that eventually occurred as well. AIG's share was one-sixth of the gains in Maiden Lane II and one-third in Maiden Lane III.

[18] See CRS Report RL34427, Financial Turmoil: Federal Reserve Policy Responses, by Marc Labonte for more information on CPFF.

[19] The CPFF interest rates ranged from 2% to 3% compared with as high as 12.5% on the regular Fed loan facility.

[20] This reporting can be found on the Federal Reserve webpage at http://www.federalreserve.gov/newsevents/ reform_cpff.htm and the figures presented here are based on this data.

[21] Preferred equity is a "hybrid" form of equity that confers no management rights with respect to the company and pays some form of dividend. It performs similarly to a loan in economic terms, but is accounted for as equity, thus improves the capital position of an institution more than a loan. As equity, preferred shares would be junior to debt, thus holdings in preferred equity would be riskier than the equivalent amount of a loan.

[22] The second large tranche of TARP assistance was used to transfer to the Treasury the AIG subsidiary equity, which the Fed had previously accepted as partial loan repayment and to partially repay the outstanding cash balance on the Fed loan.

[23] Warrants were issued in 2008 and 2009. According to AIG, "The warrant issued in 2008 provided the right to purchase approximately 2.7 million shares of AIG common stock at $50.00 per share, and the warrant issued in 2009 provided the right to purchase up to 150 shares of AIG common stock at $0.00002 per share." See http://www.aig.com/ press-releases_3171_438003.html.

[24] The IRS issued several notices on this issue, including Notice 2008-100, I.R.B. 2008-44, October 14, 2008; Notice 2009-14, I.R.B. 2009-7, January 30, 2009; Notice 2009-38, I.R.B. 2009-18, April 13, 2009; and Notice 2010-2, I.R.B. 2010-2, December 14, 2009.

[25] The tax code generally does not permit such assumption of tax losses in order to discourage companies from making acquisitions solely for the purpose of assuming tax losses.

[26] American International Group, Inc., 2011 Annual Report (SEC Form 10-K, February 23, 2012, p. 62.

[27] See, for example, http://www.treasury.gov/connect/blog/Pages/AIG-wrapup.aspx.

[28] 2 U.S.C. 661 et.seq; more information available in CRS Report RL30346, Federal Credit Reform: Implementation of the Changed Budgetary Treatment of Direct Loans and Loan Guarantees, by James M. Bickley (out of print, but available from the author). This law requires the present value of the full long-term cost of loans and loan guarantees be recognized in the federal budget when the loans or loan guarantees are made.

[29] These requirements were contained in the Emergency Economic Stabilization Act (P.L. 110-343, codified at 12 U.S.C. 5233) and apply to all TARP assistance.

[30] CBO, Report on the Troubled Asset Relief Program—May 2013, May 23, 2013, p. 6, available at http://cbo.gov/sites/ default/files/cbofiles/attachments/44256_TARP.pdf.

[31] CBO, The Budgetary Impact And Subsidy Costs Of The Federal Reserve's Actions During The Financial Crisis, May 24, 2010, p. 8, available at http://www.cbo.gov/sites/default/files/cbofiles/ftpdocs/115xx/doc11524/05-24- federalreserve.pdf.

[32] See http://www.newyorkfed.org/newsevents/news/markets/2009/an090116.html.

[33] The regulated subsidiaries were primarily the state-chartered insurance subsidiaries. Thus, if AIG had defaulted on the loan, the Fed could have seized the insurance subsidiary stock held by the holding company, but not the actual assets held by the insurance companies.

[34] Federal Reserve, "Factors Affecting Reserve Balances," Statistical Release H.4.1, September 18, 2008. See http://www.federalreserve.gov/releases/h41/20080918/; and "Report Pursuant to Section 129 of the Emergency Economic Stabilization Act of 2008: Restructuring of the Government's Financial Support to the American International Group, Inc. on November 10, 2008, p. 4. See http://www.federalreserve.gov/monetarypolicy/files/ 129aigres tructure.pdf.

[35] Terms detailed by the Federal Reserve in "Report Pursuant to Section 129 of the Emergency Economic Stabilization Act of 2008: Securities Borrowing Facility for American International Group, Inc.," available at http://www.federalreserve.gov/monetarypolicy/files/129aigsecborrowfacility.pdf.

[36] Liam Pleven et al, "AIG Bailout Hit by New Cash Woes," Wall Street Journal, October 9, 2008, p. A1.

[37] A "repo" is an agreement for the sale and repurchase of a particular security, with an overnight repo being a short term example of such a contract.

[38] N.Y. Ins. Law, Section 1410.

[39] Commercial paper is an unsecured promissory note with relatively short term maturity, typically 1 to 15 days, sold by corporations to meet immediate funding needs.

[40] American International Group, Inc., 2008 Annual Report (SEC Form 10-K), March 2, 2009.

[41] American International Group, Inc., "AIG Reports Fourth Quarter and Full Year 2009 Results," press release, February 26, 2010, p. 5, available at http://phx.corporate-ir.net/External.File?item= UGFyZW50SUQ9MzM3MjR8Q2hpbGRJ RD0tMXxUe XBlP TM=&t=1.

[42] Full details of the preferred shares can be found on the Treasury website at http://ustreas.gov/press/releases/reports/ 111008aigtermsheet.pdf.

[43] The headquarters of the Federal Reserve Bank of New York sits between Maiden Lane and Liberty Street in downtown New York City.

[44] "Maiden Lane Transactions" on the webpage of the Federal Reserve Bank of New York, available at http://www.newyorkfed.org/markets/maidenlane.html#maidenlane2.

[45] See, for example, "A.I.G. Reports Loss of $61.7 Billion as U.S. Gives More Aid," New York Times, March 2, 2009, p. A1.

[46] U.S. Treasury, "U.S. Treasury and Federal Reserve Board Announce Participation in AIG Restructuring Plan," press release, March 2, 2009.

[47] The amount was reduced from $30 billion following controversy over $165 million in employee bonuses paid to AIGFP employees in March 2009.

[48] According to The Wall Street Journal, AIG's common stock closed at a price of $39.10 on September 30, 2010.

[49] This equity was previously held by the AIG Credit Trust and was transferred to the Treasury with the dissolution of the trust.

[50] The warrants were trading for approximately $16.05 on January 20, 2011. See http://dealbook.nytimes.com/2011/01/ 20/about-a-i-g-s-stock-price/.

[51] U.S. Treasury, "Treasury to Invest in AIG Restructuring under the Emergency Economic Stabilization Act," hp-1261, November 10, 2008, available at http://www.ustreas.gov/press/releases/hp1261.htm.

[52] Section 7001 of P.L. 111-5.

[53] See "Executive Compensation" on the Treasury Financialstability.gov website available at http://www.financialstability.gov/about/executivecompensation.html.

In: Emergency Lending ...
Editor: Felicia Estrada
ISBN: 978-1-63485-393-4

Chapter 3

SYSTEMICALLY IMPORTANT OR "TOO BIG TO FAIL" FINANCIAL INSTITUTIONS*

Marc Labonte

SUMMARY

Although "too big to fail" (TBTF) has been a longstanding policy issue, it was highlighted by the near-collapse of several large financial firms in 2008. Financial firms are said to be TBTF when policy makers judge that their failure would cause unacceptable disruptions to the overall financial system, and they can be TBTF because of their size or interconnectedness. In addition to fairness issues, economic theory suggests that expectations that a firm will not be allowed to fail create moral hazard—if the creditors and counterparties of a TBTF firm believe that the government will protect them from losses, they have less incentive to monitor the firm's riskiness because they are shielded from the negative consequences of those risks. If so, they could have a funding advantage compared with other banks, which some call an implicit subsidy.

There are a number of policy approaches—some complementary, some conflicting—to coping with the TBTF problem, including providing government assistance to prevent TBTF firms from failing or systemic risk from spreading; enforcing "market discipline" to ensure that investors, creditors, and counterparties curb excessive risk-taking at

* This is an edited, reformatted and augmented version of a Congressional Research Service, Publication No. R42150, dated June 30, 2015.

TBTF firms; enhancing regulation to hold TBTF firms to stricter prudential standards than other financial firms; curbing firms' size and scope, by preventing mergers or compelling firms to divest assets, for example; minimizing spillover effects by limiting counterparty exposure; and instituting a special resolution regime for failing systemically important firms. A comprehensive policy is likely to incorporate more than one approach, as some approaches are aimed at preventing failures and some at containing fallout when a failure occurs.

Parts of the Wall Street Reform and Consumer Protection Act (Dodd-Frank Act; P.L. 111-203) address all of these policy approaches. For example, it created an enhanced prudential regulatory regime administered by the Federal Reserve for non-bank financial firms designated as "systemically important" by the Financial Stability Oversight Council (FSOC) and banks with more than $50 billion in assets. About 30 U.S. bank holding companies and a larger number of foreign banks have more than $50 billion in assets, and the FSOC has designated three insurers (AIG, MetLife, and Prudential Financial) and GE Capital as systemically important. A handful of the largest banks face additional capital, leverage, and liquidity requirements.

The Dodd-Frank Act also created a special resolution regime administered by the Federal Deposit Insurance Corporation (FDIC) to take into receivership failing firms that pose a threat to financial stability. This regime has not been used to date, and has some similarities to how the FDIC resolves failing banks. Statutory authority used to prevent financial firms from failing during the crisis has either expired or been narrowed by the Dodd-Frank Act. The fact that most large firms have grown in dollar terms since the enactment of the Dodd-Frank Act has led some critics to question whether the TBTF problem has been solved.

In the 114th Congress, S. 1484 would increase the $50 billion asset threshold to $500 billion for enhanced regulation under Title I of the Dodd-Frank Act. Banks with assets between $50 billion and $500 billion would be subject to a designation process by FSOC. Compared with the current non-bank designation process, S. 1484 would require FSOC to provide more information to (bank or non-bank) institutions and give them more opportunities to take actions to avoid or reverse systemically important financial institution (SIFI) designation. It would also increase public disclosure requirements surrounding the designation process. S.Con.Res. 11, the FY2016 budget resolution, creates a nonbinding deficit-neutral budget reserve fund that allows for future legislation "relating to any bank holding companies with over $500 billion in total assets to better protect taxpayers.... "

INTRODUCTION

Although "too big to fail" (TBTF) has been a perennial policy issue, it was highlighted by the near-collapse of several large financial firms in 2008. Large financial firms that failed or required extraordinary government assistance in the recent crisis included depositories (Citigroup and Washington Mutual), government-sponsored enterprises (Fannie Mae and Freddie Mac), insurance companies (AIG), and investment banks (Bear Stearns and Lehman Brothers).[1] In many of these cases, policymakers justified the use of government resources on the grounds that the firms were "systemically important" or "too big to fail." TBTF is the concept that a firm's disorderly failure would cause widespread disruptions in financial markets that could not easily be contained. Although the government had no explicit policy to rescue TBTF firms, several were rescued on those grounds once the crisis struck. TBTF subsequently became one of the systemic risk issues that policymakers grappled with in the wake of the recent crisis.

Systemic risk mitigation, including eliminating the TBTF problem, was a major goal of the Wall Street Reform and Consumer Protection Act (hereafter, the Dodd-Frank Act; P.L. 111-203), comprehensive financial regulatory reform enacted in 2010.[2] Different parts of this legislation jointly address the "too big to fail" problem through requirements for enhanced regulation for safety and soundness for "systemically important" (also called "systemically significant") financial institutions (SIFIs), limits on size and the types of activities a firm can engage in (including proprietary trading and hedge fund sponsorship), and the creation of a new receivership regime for resolving failing non-banks that pose systemic risk. (There has not yet been legislation enacted to reform Fannie Mae and Freddie Mac, which remain in government receivership.)

About 30 U.S. bank holding companies (BHCs) and a larger number of foreign banks are automatically subject to enhanced regulation because they have at least $50 billion in assets. In addition, the Financial Stability Oversight Council (FSOC), a council of U.S. regulators headed by the Treasury Secretary,[3] has designated three insurers (AIG, Metlife, and Prudential Financial) and one other non-bank (GE Capital) as "systemically important," and therefore subject to heightened prudential regulation.[4] MetLife has requested judicial review of its designation.[5] In April 2015, GE announced that it intended to sell most of GE Capital over the next 18 months to 24 months, in an effort, in part, to no longer be designated as systemically important.[6]

In addition, the Financial Stability Board (FSB), an international forum, has identified 30 banks, 8 of which are headquartered in the United States, as "globally systemically important banks" (GSIBs) and 9 insurers as "globally systemically important insurers," 3 of which are headquartered in the United States.[7] Under the Basel III Accord, banks identified by the FSB as systemically important are subject to higher capital standards, including capital surcharges and a higher supplementary leverage ratio.

Some critics argue that these policy reforms do not go far enough to solve the TBTF problem, and others argue it will have the perverse effect of exacerbating the TBTF problem. Ultimately, the failure of a large firm is the only test of whether the TBTF problem still exists. In the meantime, studies have found mixed evidence as to whether large financial firms can still borrow at advantageous rates compared with other firms because investors—rightly or wrongly—perceive that they enjoy TBTF status.[8]

In the 114th Congress, S. 1484, as reported by the Senate Banking Committee on June 2, 2015, would increase the $50 billion asset threshold to $500 billion for enhanced regulation under Title I of the Dodd-Frank Act. Similar to the existing non-bank designation process, banks with assets between $50 billion and $500 billion would be subject to enhanced regulation if FSOC designated them (by two-thirds vote, including the chair) as systemically important following a referral by the Fed. Compared with the current non-bank designation process, S. 1484 would require FSOC to provide more information to (bank or non-bank) institutions and give them more opportunities to take actions to avoid or reverse SIFI designation. It would increase public disclosure requirements surrounding the designation process. S.Con.Res. 11, the FY2016 budget resolution, creates a nonbinding deficit-neutral budget reserve fund that allows for future legislation "relating to any bank holding companies with over $500 billion in total assets to better protect taxpayers...."

This report discusses the economic issues raised by TBTF, broad policy options, and policy changes made by the relevant Dodd-Frank provisions. This report also discusses recent legislation addressing the TBTF issue in the 114th Congress. The report ends with an **Appendix** reviewing the historical experience with TBTF before and during the recent crisis.

ECONOMIC ISSUES

Context

Evidence on the size of financial firms can be viewed in absolute and relative terms—relative to other industries and within the industry (i.e., concentration). In the first quarter of 2015, there were 38 U.S. banks with more than $50 billion in assets, of which four had more than $1.5 trillion in assets. In 2003, there was only one U.S. bank with more than $1 trillion in assets.[9]

In recent decades, the U.S. banking industry has become more concentrated, meaning that a greater percentage of total industry assets is held by large banks. Assets of the five largest BHCs totaled 52% of total BHC assets as of June 30, 2014.[10] According to one study, the three largest banks held 5% to 15% of total commercial banking depository assets from the 1930s until the 1990s. The share of the top three then rose until it had reached about 40% by 2008.[11] By international standards, U.S. banks are not that large, however. Relative to GDP, the combined assets of the top three U.S. banks were the lowest of any major OECD economy in 2009.[12]

The four largest BHCs each held a majority of their assets in commercial bank subsidiaries. Not all very large financial institutions are commercial banks, however. Companies with more than $100 billion in assets include insurers, broker-dealers, investment funds, specialized lenders, and government-sponsored enterprises (Fannie Mae and Freddie Mac are among the largest firms overall by assets). Over the long run, large non-banks have emerged, in part because of the growth in "shadow banking."[13] Shadow banking refers to bank-like activities, such as lending, in the non-bank financial sector.[14] According to one estimate, assets of broker-dealers grew from 3% of commercial bank assets in 1980 to nearly 30% in 2007. Over the same period, hedge fund capital increased from less than 1% of bank capital to more than 100%.[15] While non-banks have been engaging in more bank-like activities, banks have also moved into non-banking businesses. Today, a bank can incorporate as a financial holding company that has depository subsidiaries, insurance subsidiaries, and broker-dealer subsidiaries, for example.

The financial crisis reduced the number of large financial firms, but also led to an increase in the size of the remaining large firms, through a series of mergers and acquisitions.[16]

Compared with other industries, financial firms are large in dollar terms when measured by assets and liabilities, but not by measures such as revenue because of the nature of financial intermediation. For example, there are only two firms (Berkshire Hathaway and General Electric) with revenues from financial businesses—and both have substantial non-financial revenues—and no BHCs among the 10 largest Fortune 500 firms in 2015 when measured by revenue, but financial companies are the only Fortune 500 firms in the top 10 for assets or with more than $1 trillion in assets.[17] Financial firms are also not as concentrated as some other industries.[18] In layman's terms, there is no "Pepsi/Coke" dominance in the financial sector. These comparisons may help to illustrate why traditional policy tools such as antitrust have not been used against large financial firms recently and suggest that the TBTF phenomenon in finance lies in the nature of financial intermediation, which is the topic of the next section.

Economic Effects of Too Big to Fail

Contagion can be transmitted from small or large financial institutions (see the following text box), but large firms pose unique problems. Firms are likely to have more counterparty exposure to large firms, and the losses or disruptions caused by counterparty exposure when a large firm fails could be severe enough to lead to failure of third parties. Problems at large firms could also lead to "fire sales" in specific securities markets that depress market prices, thereby imposing losses on other holders of similar securities.[19] Some economists argue that the real problem is some firms are "too interconnected to fail." That is, it is not the sheer size of certain firms that causes contagion, but the fact that most activity in certain key market segments flows through those firms.[20] According to the International Monetary Fund (IMF), a few large firms "dominate key market segments ranging from private securitization and derivatives dealing to triparty repo and leveraged investor financing."[21] Were the interconnected firm to fail, other firms would have difficulty absorbing the failed firm's business, and there would be disruptions to the flow of credit. If problems in one market segment undermine an interconnected firm, problems can spread to the other market segments in which the firm operates.

Why Are Financial Firms Vulnerable to Instability?

Economists consider financial firms to be uniquely vulnerable to instability because a fundamental feature of financial intermediation is the use of short-term liabilities (debt or deposits) to finance long-term assets (e.g., loans). As a result, assets cannot be liquidated fast enough or at a sufficient price to fund redemptions in a panic. The use of liabilities, rather than equity, to finance most assets (referred to as "leverage") can result in losses exceeding equity, which results in insolvency, or an inability to meet obligations to all creditors in full. These features make financial intermediaries inherently vulnerable to runs—since those who redeem funds first are thought more likely to access their funds, there is an incentive for creditors to rush to redeem, whether the firm is suffering from a liquidity problem or a solvency problem. Panics can be self-fulfilling: whether or not the institution originally had financial problems, a panic can lead to its failure. Panics are also prone to contagion—the observation of a run at one institution can lead creditors to run on other institutions, because of perceived connections or similarities to the original firm.

The classic run involves depositors at banks, but the recent crisis demonstrated that other debt markets can also be susceptible to runs for banks and non-bank financial firms. Non-bank financial firms were highly reliant on short-term borrowing, through financial instruments such as repurchase agreements and commercial paper. They favor short-term borrowing because in normal conditions these short-term funds are inexpensive and readily available. The short maturity of these instruments meant that loans needed to be rolled over frequently. The proximate cause of most of these firms' failure was the inability to roll over maturing debt. When these firms experienced financial difficulties, counterparties became reluctant (or were not in a position) to transact and maintain business relationships with them. For example, major investment banks are "market-makers" (ready buyers and sellers) for securities markets; provide prime brokerage services for hedge funds; are major participants in over-the-counter markets for securities such as derivatives; play important roles in payment, clearing, and settlement activities; and so on. If counterparties in any of these areas are no longer willing to transact with the firm because of fears of a run, the firm's financial difficulties can quickly compound.

Although some policy makers have dismissed the claim that any firm could be too big to fail, many analysts believe the failure of Lehman Brothers, occurring in the context of difficulties at several large financial firms, was the proximate cause of the worsening of the crisis in September 2008.[22] It is debatable whether policy actions in the months leading up to Lehman Brothers' failure made its failure more or less disruptive, but it is fair to say that it is unlikely that the panic that followed could have been avoided since the nature of the disruptions its failure caused (notably, its effect on money markets) was not widely foreseen.[23] "Bailing out" TBTF firms may not be an intended policy objective, but may become the second-best crisis containment measure when the failure of a TBTF firm is imminent to prevent fallout to the broader financial system and the economy as a whole.

While many people object to rescuing TBTF firms on moral or philosophical grounds, there are also economic reasons why having firms that are TBTF is inefficient. In general, for market forces to lead to an efficient allocation of resources, finding a good use of resources must be financially rewarded and a bad use must be financially punished. Firms generally run into financial problems when they have persistently allocated capital to inefficient uses. To save such a firm would be expected to retard efforts to shift that capital to more efficient uses, and may allow the firm to continue making more bad decisions in the future. The TBTF problem results in too much financial intermediation taking place at large firms and too little at other firms from the perspective of economic efficiency, although not necessarily from the perspective of noneconomic policy rationales.[24] Because large and small financial firms do not serve exactly the same customers or operate in exactly the same lines of business, too much capital will flow to the customers and in the lines of business of large firms and too little to those of small firms in the presence of TBTF.

Preventing TBTF firms from failing is argued to be necessary for maintaining the stability of the financial system in the short run. But rescuing TBTF firms is predicted to lead to a less stable financial system in the long run because of moral hazard that weakens market discipline. Moral hazard refers to the theory that if TBTF firms expect that failure will be prevented, they have an incentive to take greater risks than they otherwise would because they are shielded from at least some negative consequences of those risks.[25] In general, riskier investments have a higher rate of return to compensate for the greater risk of failure. If TBTF firms believe that they will not be allowed to fail, then private firms capture any additional profits that result from high-risk activities, while the government bears any extreme losses. Thus, if TBTF firms believe that they will be rescued, they have an incentive to behave in a way that makes it more likely they will fail.

To see how the moral hazard problem is transmitted, it is helpful to examine who gets directly "rescued" when the government intervenes to prevent the fallout to the overall financial system and broader economy. The direct beneficiaries of a rescue will include some combination of the firm's management, owners (e.g., shareholders), creditors (including depositors), account holders, and counterparties. Under bankruptcy, these groups would bear losses to differing degrees depending on the legal priority of their claims. Government assistance, depending on its terms, can protect some or all of these groups from losses. In some recent government rescues, management has been replaced; in others, it has not. Even if management believes that losses will lead to removal, managers may prefer excessive risk taking (with higher expected profits) because they are not personally liable for the firms' losses.[26] In some cases, shareholders have borne some losses through stock dilution, although their losses may have been smaller than they would have been in a bankruptcy. Creditors, account holders, and counterparties have generally been shielded from any losses. Thus, government rescues have not mitigated the moral hazard problem for creditors and counterparties. Because the government will only intervene in the case of extreme losses, moral hazard may manifest itself primarily in areas affected only by systemic events (referred to as "tail risk"). For example, extreme losses from counterparty risk may be ignored by counterparties to TBTF firms if they believe that government will always intervene to prevent failure; if so, costs (such as the amount of margin a counterparty will require) will be lower for TBTF firms than competitors in these markets.

Do TBTF Firms Enjoy a Funding Advantage or Implicit Subsidy?

Economic theory predicts that in the presence of moral hazard, creditors and counterparties of TBTF firms provide credit at an inefficiently low cost. Some studies have provided evidence that the funding advantage exists, although many of these studies cover time periods that end before the enactment of the Dodd-Frank Act.[27] Identifying a lower funding cost for large banks alone is not enough to prove a moral hazard effect because lower cost could also be due to other factors, such as greater liquidity or lower risk (e.g., greater diversity).[28] A Government Accountability Office (GAO) review of the empirical literature found that a funding advantage for large firms during the financial crisis had declined by 2011. Its own econometric analysis found evidence of a funding advantage during the crisis, but mixed evidence on the existence of a funding advantage in 2012 and 2013—indeed, more versions of their model found higher funding costs for large banks rather than the expected lower costs, holding other factors equal.[29]

Some view the decision by certain credit rating agencies to rate the largest financial firms more highly because they assume the firms would receive government support as evidence of the funding advantage, although two of the three major rating agencies have reduced the magnitude of this "ratings uplift" in recent years.[30] (It should be noted that credit ratings do not directly determine funding costs.)

This funding advantage is sometimes referred to as the TBTF subsidy, although a subsidy typically implies a government willingness to provide the recipient with a benefit. Note also that a subsidy typically takes the form of an explicit direct payment, financial support, or guarantee, whereas in this case, if the funding advantage exists, it would derive from the expectation of future support that has not been pledged.

POLICY OPTIONS

Policy Before and during the Crisis

TBTF policy before the crisis could be described as purposeful ambiguity—policy was not explicit about what would happen in the event that large financial firms become insolvent, or which firms were considered TBTF.[31] (Certain statutory benefits conferred to Fannie Mae and Freddie Mac came closer to an explicit TBTF status, and markets treated them as such.) Conventional wisdom before the crisis was that this ambiguity would help contain the moral hazard problem—if investors and creditors did not know if a firm was TBTF, they would err on the side of caution and treat it as if it were not TBTF.[32] Problems with large firms in the recent crisis suggest that this approach was not effective.

Theoretically, moral hazard can be mitigated through prudential regulation for safety and soundness. Generally, the regulatory regime before the crisis was not based on firm size, but rather on charter type. Depository institutions were regulated for safety and soundness to minimize the costs of, and the moral hazard that results from, deposit insurance and access to the Fed's discount window. Because some non-bank financial firms did not receive analogous government protection before the crisis, there was not seen to be a moral hazard problem that justified regulating them for safety and soundness. Pre-crisis safety and soundness regulation did not explicitly address the additional moral hazard that results from TBTF, in part because TBTF firms were not explicitly identified.

Before the crisis, large financial firms were subject to Federal Reserve (Fed) prudential oversight at the holding company level if they were organized as BHCs or financial holding companies.[33] Prudential regulation entailed supervision and examination for safety and soundness. In 1997, the Fed and the Office of the Comptroller of the Currency (OCC) set up an internal team to supervise large complex banking organizations.[34] Regulation at the holding company level did not mean that all subsidiaries were regulated for safety and soundness by the Fed. BHCs could operate non-banking subsidiaries, but banking regulators could only regulate banking subsidiaries for safety and soundness. "Firewalls" were meant to protect the depository subsidiary from losses at other types of subsidiaries. The holding company had to demonstrate that it was a source of strength for the depository subsidiary.[35] Government-sponsored enterprises, such as Fannie Mae, Freddie Mac, and the Federal Home Loan Banks, were also subject to prudential regulation by their own regulators. Prudential regulation did not prevent all large banks or the GSEs from experiencing financial difficulties during the crisis.

Some of the large firms that experienced financial difficulties in the recent crisis, however, were not BHCs, under Fed regulation, at that time. Types of large firms that were not BHCs included some government sponsored enterprises, insurance companies, investment banks (or broker-dealers), and hedge funds. Insurance subsidiaries were regulated for safety and soundness at the state level. Investment banks complied with an SEC net capital rule. Some large financial firms, including AIG and Lehman Brothers, were thrift holding companies supervised by the Office of Thrift Supervision before the crisis. The Office of Thrift Supervision was mainly concerned with the health of AIG's and Lehman Brothers' thrift subsidiaries, although those were a minor part of their businesses.

Some large financial firms voluntarily became BHCs during the crisis. Specifically, the five largest investment banks either merged with BHCs (Bear Stearns, Merrill Lynch), became BHCs (Goldman Sachs, Morgan Stanley), or declared bankruptcy (Lehman Brothers) in 2008.

If a bank is heading toward insolvency, the FDIC normally takes it into receivership and resolves it. Statutory requirements of least cost resolution of failing depositories by the FDIC may also help to minimize moral hazard, because bailing out firms (i.e., making creditors whole) is often more costly than shutting a firm down. But least cost resolution could be waived by the Treasury Secretary, upon the recommendation of the FDIC and Federal

Reserve, if a systemic risk exception were invoked.[36] Market participants may have expected that the systemic risk exception would be invoked for large firms. The presumption before the crisis was that a failed non-bank would be subject to the standard corporate bankruptcy process; there was no standing policy of government involvement in the failure of a non-bank, with the exception of conservatorship authority for Fannie Mae and Freddie Mac.[37]

The Federal Reserve was authorized to provide liquidity to banks through collateralized loans at the discount window, with limitations for banks that are not well capitalized. In previous episodes of financial turmoil such as 1987 and 1998, the Fed's decision to flood markets with liquidity had proven sufficient to restore confidence.[38] There was no standing policy to provide liquidity to non-bank financial firms to guard against runs before the recent crisis. Such a policy did not prove necessary to maintain stability before the recent crisis, perhaps because there was less historical experience with non-bank runs, and perhaps because non-bank financial firms have become a more important part of the financial system over time. The Fed had broad existing emergency authority under Section 13(3) of the Federal Reserve Act to lend to non-banks, but prior to the crisis had not done so since the 1930s.

Policy during the recent crisis could be described as reactive, developing ad hoc in fits and starts in reaction to events. Ultimately, banks received federal assistance, and a lack of an explicit safety net and federal prudential regulation did not prevent some non-banks from receiving federal assistance as well. In the absence of explicit authority to rescue a TBTF firm, as the crisis unfolded, the broad standing authority was used: Section 13(3) was used to prevent the failures of Bear Stearns and AIG. Section 13(3) and the FDIC's systemic risk authority[39] was used to offer asset guarantees to Bank of America and Citigroup. These authorities were also used to create broadly based emergency programs. Other programs were created after the crisis began under authority granted by Congress in 2008. Assistance was given under the Housing and Economic Recovery Act (HERA; P.L. 110-289) to prevent Fannie Mae and Freddie Mac from becoming insolvent. In October 2008, Congress passed the Emergency Economic Stabilization Act (EESA; P.L. 110-343), creating the Troubled Asset Relief Program (TARP), which was used, among other things, to inject capital into several large financial firms.[40] The Fed and FDIC authorities are permanent; as discussed below, both authorities were modified by the Dodd-Frank Act. The HERA and EESA authority expired in 2010, although funds continued to be available after expiration under several outstanding contracts.

Policy Options and the Policy Response after the Crisis

Policy options for TBTF can be categorized as preventive (how to prevent TBTF firms from either emerging or posing systemic risk) or reactive (how to contain the fallout when a TBTF firm experiences a crisis). A comprehensive policy is likely to incorporate more than one approach because different approaches are aimed at different parts of the problem. A policy approach that would not solve the TBTF problem in isolation could be successful in conjunction with others. Some policy approaches are complementary—others could counteract each other.

Although there are costs to having large financial firms because of the moral hazard problems, these costs must be weighed against potential benefits to determine the economically optimal policy response. These benefits are discussed in the section below entitled "Limiting the Size of Financial Firms."

When considering each policy option discussed in this section, an alternative perspective to consider is that problems at large firms during the crisis—such as overleveraging, a sudden loss of liquidity, concentrated or undiversified losses, investor uncertainty caused by opacity—were not TBTF problems per se. If, in fact, they were representative of problems that firms of all sizes were experiencing, policy should directly treat these problems in a systematic and uniform way for all firms, and not just for TBTF firms, in this view. In other words, prudential regulation, a special resolution regime, and policies limiting spillover effects could be applied to all firms operating in a given area rather than just large firms, so arguments for and against these policy options do not apply only to their application to large firms. If the causes of systemic risk are not tied to firm size or interconnectedness, then policies based on differential treatment of TBTF firms could result in systemic risk migrating to non-TBTF firms rather than being eliminated.

End or Continue "Bailouts"?

Options

"Bailouts" are defined differently by different people. For the purposes of this report, they are defined as government assistance to a single firm to prevent it from failing (i.e., allow it to meet all ongoing obligations in full), in contrast to widely available emergency government programs to provide liquidity to solvent firms. TBTF bailouts could be delivered through assistance unique to the firm or through existing government programs on a preferential, subsidized basis.[41] They could come in the form of federal loans, insurance, guarantees, capital injections, or other firm-specific commitments.

Three broad policy approaches to government "bailouts" of failing TBTF firms are available: (1) institutionalize the availability of assistance in standing programs with standards and procedures for access enumerated beforehand; (2) offer assistance on an ad hoc basis using broad, discretionary authority, adding authority as necessary; or (3) eliminate any source of broad authority that could potentially make assistance available (often referred to as a "market discipline" policy).

The policy approach pursued before and during the crisis was essentially the second, as discussed in the previous section. The crisis left many policy makers and observers criticizing this approach as arbitrary, unfair, lacking in transparency, and too costly (although, in most cases, funds were eventually repaid in full).[42] Many economists would also credit it with eventually restoring financial stability, however, by restoring healthy and unhealthy financial firms' access to liquidity and capital.[43]

One problem with a "bailouts" approach is that one can only learn whether a firm's failure would be disruptive if it is allowed to fail. Once a firm has been rescued, there is no way of knowing how disruptive its failure would have been. As a result, policy makers may decide to err on the side of caution and rescue any firm that they believe poses risk of contagion since the short-term costs of disruption to financial markets may be high. In this sense, the number of firms that are politically TBTF, particularly at times of market stress, may be larger than the number that are economically TBTF (i.e., pose systemic risk).

Under the market discipline approach, policy makers would pledge to provide no federal assistance to any failing firm going forward. In theory, if creditors believed that a firm would not receive government support, they would not enable firms to take what they perceived to be excessive risks, and risky actions would be priced more efficiently.[44] Unfortunately, accomplishing this goal is not as simple as proclaiming a "no bailouts" policy. If the moral hazard problem is to be avoided, market participants must be convinced that when faced with a failure that could potentially be highly damaging to the broader economy—and just how damaging cannot be fully known until after the fact—policy makers will not deviate from the stated policy and provide bailouts. But current policy makers cannot prevent future policy makers from offering assistance to a failing TBTF firm. Although it is in the long-term interest of policy makers to withhold assistance to prevent moral hazard, it is in the short-term interest of policy makers to provide assistance to prevent systemic risk. This makes it difficult to craft a "market discipline" policy that is credible to market participants.[45] Even if policy makers did intend to maintain a market discipline policy, as long as creditors disbelieved such a policy would be maintained in the event of a crisis, the moral hazard problem would remain.

Events in the crisis rewarded size and interconnectedness and arguably made any future "market discipline" policy approach less credible. As discussed in the **Appendix**, widespread financial assistance was provided in 2007-2009 to large institutions, although official policy prior to the crisis could have been construed as a "no bailouts" policy. Creditors may view the 2007-2009 policy response as the most likely outcome in future systemic risk episodes. According to the Congressional Oversight Panel, "In light of these events, it is not surprising that markets have incorporated the notion that 'too big to fail' banks are safer than their 'small enough to fail' counterparts."[46] An alternative perspective is that market participants may view public dissatisfaction with the 2007-2009 policy response as making a repeat unlikely.

Although it is impossible to prevent future policy makers from making statutory changes to current policy, current policy makers can make it more difficult for future policy makers to "bail out" firms by repealing or limiting the existing standing authority that policy makers used to provide assistance in the crisis. Enacting new authority is likely to be a higher hurdle than invoking existing authority. Examples of standing authority include the Fed's 13(3) emergency authority and the FDIC's systemic risk exception to least cost resolution. The advantage to maintaining broad discretionary emergency authority is that it allows policy makers to react quickly to unforeseen contingencies, and the authority may be used for other purposes than bailouts, as defined in this report. If assistance became necessary in a fast-moving crisis, new authority might take too long to enact. By then, the damage to the economy could be worse. In other words, eliminating broad authority could still result in a TBTF rescue, but after more financial disruption had occurred. TARP is an example of authority that was enacted relatively quickly during a crisis; nevertheless, its enactment took weeks, whereas contagion can spread in days.

If one believes that assistance is inevitable because of short-term incentives, there are two advantages to institutionalizing the terms of assistance. First, making the terms and conditions explicit reduces the likelihood that assistance could be provided arbitrarily or on the basis of favoritism, and provides an opportunity to create a funding mechanism so that funding is not shifted to the taxpayer. Second, an explicit policy avoids policy uncertainty, which can heighten systemic risk. Arguably, lack of explicit policy added to the panic after Lehman Brothers failed, because market participants may have incorrectly based decisions on the expectation that Lehman Brothers would receive the same type of government assistance that Bear Stearns received.[47] A drawback is that setting forth standards for coping with problems at large firms before the fact could make the moral hazard problem worse by leaving no ambiguity about which firms will receive assistance.

A related approach would be to allow TBTF firms to fail, but stop contagion by creating standing credit facilities ahead of time to aid solvent counterparties. This would reduce moral hazard on the firm's part (because its managers would have a greater incentive to avoid failure), but would not eliminate it because counterparties would have less reason to monitor the firm's riskiness. An example of this approach is the decision to let Lehman Brothers fail, then subsequently offer a blanket guarantee for money market mutual funds (MMFs) to prevent a run triggered by one such fund's financial difficulties related to its holdings of Lehman debt.[48] As the MMF example illustrates, sometimes this approach could require assistance to be extended much more broadly than to just direct counterparties. Further, if standing facilities are too easily accessed, they could crowd out private inter-firm lending.

The optimal approach to bailouts from an economic perspective is arguably the one that is least costly to the economy in the short and long run. The cost of TBTF to the economy includes the direct expenditures by the government and the costs of a less stable financial system due to moral hazard. It can be argued that a failure to bail out TBTF firms would make the system less stable, because it would potentially allow systemic risk to spread. Alternatively, if bailouts increase moral hazard, it can be argued that greater moral hazard causes the system to be less stable by encouraging TBTF firms to act less prudently. However, even without moral hazard, firms would sometimes fail, as finance is inherently risky.

The 2008 experience lacks a counterfactual to definitively answer the question of which approach is least costly in the short run. The crisis worsened after Lehman Brothers was allowed to fail and ended after TARP and other broadly based emergency programs were created. Ad hoc rescues of failing TBTF firms had not succeeded in stabilizing financial markets to that point, but it is unknown whether financial conditions would have eventually normalized had that ad hoc policy been pursued consistently and continually.

There is also no counterfactual as to what would have happened if there had been a consistent policy of allowing firms to fail in the crisis dating back to Bear Stearns, but the outcome that policy makers believed would occur if Bear Stearns had not been rescued is similar to events following the Lehman Brothers bankruptcy.

During the crisis, it appeared that the ultimate cost to the government of TBTF "bailouts" could run into the hundreds of billions, collectively.[49] In hindsight, all of the special assistance to large financial firms (Bear Stearns, the GSEs, Ally Financial, Chrysler Financial, AIG, Citigroup, and Bank of America), as well as the broadly based emergency programs that large and small financial firms accessed, turned out to be cash-flow positive for the government (i.e., income and principal repayments exceeded outlays).[50] Cash-flow measures, however, do not reflect the economic cost of assistance, which would factor in the rate of return a private investor would have required to make a similar investment, incorporating risk and the time value of money. On an economic basis, CBO has estimated that special assistance through TARP to Citigroup, Bank of America, the auto financing firms, and broadly based programs have generated positive profits for the government, while the TARP assistance to AIG was subsidized.[51] Although there were ultimately no net losses in these cases, these government interventions exposed the government to large potential losses.

Estimates of the cost to the government of "bailouts" do not include the broader costs of a systemic disruption to the economy, which would have feedback effects on the federal budget. In this sense, the question of whether it is more costly to bail out TBTF firms or allow them to fail cannot be definitively settled. Arguably, it was the government's interventions following Lehman Brothers' collapse that ultimately ended the panic, as measured by standard measures of financial stress such as the spread between Treasury rates and the London Inter-bank Offering Rate (LIBOR), which did not begin to fall until legislation creating TARP was enacted.[52]

Policy Response

Maintaining broad discretionary authority, but attempting to limit its scope to prevent bailing out insolvent firms could be seen as the approach taken by Title XI of the Dodd-Frank Act. It limits the Fed to providing emergency assistance only through widely available facilities, requires the Fed to issue rules and regulations on how such assistance will be provided, and prohibits the Fed from lending to failing firms.[53] It also created new statutory authority for the FDIC to set up emergency liquidity programs in the future with restrictions and limitations, including that the recipient must be solvent, rather than allowing the FDIC to again rely on an open-ended systemic risk exception. Critics would argue that emergency authority remains broad enough under the Dodd-Frank Act that regulators would be likely to use it to save TBTF firms in the future. The Dodd-Frank Act did not institutionalize a broadly based capital injection program similar to TARP's Capital Purchase Program, which expired in 2010.

Limiting the Size of Financial Firms

Options

One approach to eliminating TBTF is to alter the characteristics of firms that make them TBTF. If TBTF is primarily a function of size, policy makers could require TBTF firms to sell businesses, divest assets, or break up to the point that they are no longer TBTF. Size can be measured in different ways, and regulators would likely need to use discretion to weigh a number of measures.[54] It is also not obvious at what size a firm becomes a source of systemic risk—should the line be drawn at, say, $1 trillion, $100 billion, or $50 billion of assets?—and could not be confirmed until firms failed. A firm could be TBTF because of its overall size or because of its size or importance in a particular segment of the financial market, suggesting that overall size alone may not be a sufficient determinant of systemic importance. It is also possible that if all institutions were smaller because of a size cap, the largest institutions would still be systemically important, even though their size would not be large by today's standards. A parallel might be the decision to rescue Continental Illinois in 1984—it was the seventh-largest bank, but had assets of only $45 billion at its peak, as geographic restrictions meant that the average size of all banks was smaller.[55]

The benefits of reducing the size of firms are that, if successful, it could eliminate the moral hazard and the need for future "bailouts" stemming from TBTF. Other potential costs and benefits are more ambiguous. Size restrictions may raise the cost or reduce the quality of financial products currently provided by TBTF firms to consumers and investors; whether this is good or bad from an economic perspective depends on the cause. If low costs currently stem primarily from the TBTF "subsidy," then economic efficiency would improve if large firms are eliminated even if costs rose as a result.[56] Alternatively, if low costs currently stem primarily from economies of scale, then economic efficiency would be reduced by size restrictions.[57] Beyond cost, large firms may make markets more liquid and enhance customer convenience (such as a nationwide physical presence). Large non-financial firms may also have financial needs (such as the underwriting of securities) that would overwhelm small financial firms.[58] Similarly, if the success of the largest firms comes primarily through their ability to innovate and provide more sophisticated or superior products, then size restrictions could reduce economic efficiency.[59] Alternatively, if success of large firms comes primarily through the ability to extract monopoly rents, size restrictions could improve economic efficiency.[60] While reducing size should reduce systemic risk, there is mixed evidence on whether large firms are more or less likely to fail than small firms.[61] They could be less likely to fail because of greater diversification or more sophisticated risk management. Canada's unique experience in avoiding the recent financial crisis is attributed by some to its highly concentrated banking system.[62]

Unless rules to limit the size of financial firms are global, size restrictions could place U.S. firms at a disadvantage at home and abroad in their competition with foreign financial firms. (Some types of financial activities can be performed abroad more easily than others, so the relevance of this factor depends on the activity in question.) If business were to shift to large foreign firms, the overall level of systemic risk in the financial system (which already involves large international capital flows) may not decline, or could even increase if prudential regulation in the foreign firm's home country were inferior to U.S. regulation.

An alternative to restricting size would be to penalize size through a tax or assessment on assets or liabilities above a stated threshold. In theory, the tax could be set at the rate that would neutralize any funding advantage that a bank enjoys because of its TBTF status. Given that it is uncertain at what size a financial firm becomes TBTF, a tax could be viewed as less harmful than a cap if set at the wrong threshold and perhaps more easily adjusted over time. Other policy options that raise funding costs for large firms, such as higher capital requirements, can be viewed as having a similar effect to a tax.[63]

If policy makers decided to reduce the size of firms, a phase-in or transition period might be desirable to avoid significant short-term disruptions to the overall financial system. Likewise, when designing a policy that applies only to firms above a size threshold, one consideration is whether to make the threshold graduated to avoid cliff effects. Otherwise, firms might take actions to remain just below the threshold.

Policy Response

Section 121 of the Dodd-Frank Act allows the Federal Reserve to prevent mergers and acquisitions, restrict the products a firm is allowed to offer, terminate activities, and sell assets if the Federal Reserve and at least two-thirds of the Financial Stability Oversight Council believes that a firm that has more than $50 billion in assets poses a "grave threat to the financial stability of the United States." It does not allow the Fed to undertake these actions simply because a firm is large.

Before the crisis, a BHC was limited to holding no more than 10% of national deposits and 30% of any state's deposits. Section 622 of the Dodd-Frank Act prevents mergers or consolidations that would result in a firm with more than 10% of total liabilities of certain financial firms or, in the case of a bank, 10% of the total amount of deposits of insured depository institutions in the United States. This limit can be waived in the case of the acquisition of a failing firm. The limit does not prevent firms from increasing their market share "organically."[64] The FSOC has determined that Section 622 will limit the acquisitions of only the four largest BHCs at this time.[65]

The Dodd-Frank Act allowed fees to be assessed on banks with more than $50 billion in assets and non-banks designated as systemically important. The fees were intended to finance the costs of supervision and resolution, as well as the budget of the Office of Financial Research, as opposed to being punitive, however.

Limiting the Scope of Financial Firms

Options

The activities in which bank subsidiaries may engage are restricted by statute, but bank holding companies may own non-bank subsidiaries.[66] The subsidiaries of, and off-balance sheet entities associated with, the largest BHCs are active participants, to varying degrees, in multiple lines of business outside of traditional bank lending, including asset-backed securitization, trust services, insurance, money market mutual funds, and broker-dealers.[67] A large firm's presence throughout the financial system is one source of its "interconnectedness."

Imposing a size restriction on firms is relatively straightforward—it requires establishing a measure of size, identifying the threshold size that makes a firm TBTF, and preventing firms from exceeding that threshold. Altering firms so that they are not too interconnected to fail is more complicated because there is less consensus on what characteristics make a firm "too interconnected."[68] If interconnectedness is taken to mean that the firm is an important participant in several different segments of financial markets, then policy makers could take what has popularly been described as the "reinstate Glass-Steagall" approach.[69] The essence of this proposal is to prevent a single financial holding company from operating in multiple lines of financial business, echoing Glass-Steagall's separation of banking and investing.[70] Reintroducing the separation of lines of business alone would not necessarily prevent the existence of very large or interconnected firms within a market segment, however, in which case the TBTF problem would not be eliminated.

The benefits of reducing the scope of firms are that, if successful, it could reduce the riskiest activities of large firms and thus the need for future "bailouts" stemming from TBTF. It could also reduce the complexity of large firms, making it easier for regulators and creditors to monitor them. Weighed against those benefits would be a number of costs.

First, there may be economies of scope that make the financial system more efficient and complete if firms are large, diversified, and interconnected. Customers may benefit from the convenience, sophistication, and savings of "one-stop shopping" and expertise in multiple market segments.

Second, large firms that operate in multiple lines of business may be better able to reduce risk through diversification, making them less prone to instability in that sense. Traditional banking is not inherently safe, so forbidding banks from engaging in other activities is no panacea to avoid bank failures. Fannie Mae and Freddie Mac are examples of firms that were deemed "too big to fail" and rescued on those grounds although their business was narrowly focused in the mortgage market.

Third, reintroducing Glass-Steagall separations of businesses without other changes to the regulatory system would reinforce a system in which banking is subject to close federal prudential regulation and other financial firms are not. This system would only mitigate systemic risk if non-banking activities and institutions could not be a source of systemic risk—the recent crisis experience casts doubt on that assumption. Further, the growth in "shadow banking" makes it more difficult to segregate activities and their regulation by charter—financial innovation has blurred the distinction between different lines of business in finance to the point where the distinction may not be meaningful. In other words, some activities of non-banks are not fundamentally different from core banking activities from an economic perspective. Thus, the activities that banks could undertake would be limited, but it would be difficult to prevent non-banks from engaging in bank-like activities with the same implications for systemic risk, but less or no prudential regulation. Similar arguments apply to the potential for activities to migrate abroad, where "universal banking" is common.

Another policy approach would be to limit or ban TBTF firms' participation in activities that are deemed inherently too risky—particularly those likely to generate large losses at times of financial stress—and not central to the business model of the firm. This approach usually focuses on banks because of their access to the "federal safety net" (deposit insurance and Fed lending), and hence justified in terms of limiting risk to taxpayers. For example, many policy makers have argued that banks should not participate in proprietary trading of private securities with the bank's own funds.[71] Although all financial activities are risky, some risks can be more easily managed through techniques such as hedging and supervised by regulators. Whether proprietary trading is an inherently riskier activity than other banking functions, such as lending, is subject to debate. In addition to proprietary trading, Thomas Hoenig and Charles Morris have proposed to also ban banks from acting as broker-dealers and market-makers in securities and derivatives.[72]

Another variation of this proposal, made by the Vickers Commission in the United Kingdom[73] and the Liikanen Group in the European Union,[74] is to "ring fence" banking activities from these other types of activities into legally, financially, and operationally separate entities within a holding company structure.[75] This type of approach can be seen in U.S. policies to move swap dealer activities outside of the depository subsidiary and into a separately capitalized subsidiary (referred to as "the swap push out rule").[76] Similarly to proprietary trading, a challenge to this approach is to differentiate between derivatives activities that regulators want depository subsidiaries to engage in, such as risk-mitigating hedging, and the targeted activities, such as swap dealing.

Although proposals limiting scope would apply to both large and small banks, some are likely to have a greater impact on large firms. For example, Bloomberg Government estimates that over 99% of trading assets and liabilities are held by 25 banks.[77]

A drawback to limiting permissible activities is that there is unlikely to be any sharp distinction between the risky activity and similar activities that are central to the firm's core activities. As a result, regulators may have to make arbitrary distinctions between which activities fall under the ban, and firms would have an incentive to skirt the ban by designing transactions that resemble allowed activities but accomplish the same goals as the banned activity. For example, proprietary trading ("playing the market" with a firm's own assets) may be hard to distinguish from market-making (providing clients with a ready buyer and seller of securities) or hedging (buying and selling securities such as derivatives to reduce risk), and there may be economies of scale to market-making that concentrate those activities at large firms.[78] Finally, risky activities may still be a source of systemic risk even if banks or TBTFs are banned from conducting them.

Policy Response

Section 619 of the Dodd-Frank Act, popularly referred to as the "Volcker Rule," prohibits banks from engaging in proprietary trading and owning hedge funds and private equity funds in the United States, and requires additional capital to be held by systemically important non-banks that engage in proprietary trading or own hedge funds and private equity funds in the United States.[79] Insurance companies are largely excluded from the Volcker Rule. Exemptions from the Volcker Rule include the purchase and sale of assets for purposes of underwriting, market making, hedging, and on behalf of clients. Securities issued by federal, state, or local governments and government-sponsored enterprises (GSEs) are exempted, as are investments in small business investment companies. A final rule implementing the Volcker Rule was adopted in December 2013, with conformance required by June 2015.[80] Small banks have argued that since activities prohibited by the Volcker Rule are performed primarily at large banks, small banks should be exempted from it.

Section 716 of the Dodd-Frank Act requires banks to "push out" certain swap dealer activities into separately capitalized affiliates.[81] The stated goal of the provision is to prevent swap dealers and major swap participants from accessing deposit insurance or the Fed's discount window. The rule implementing Section 716 was effective July 2013, with a two-year transition period.[82] A provision in the FY2015 appropriations bill (P.L. 113-235) limited the scope of the pushout rule.[83]

Regulating TBTF

Options

Another approach to addressing the TBTF problem takes as its starting point that no policy can prevent TBTF firms from emerging. In this view, the dominant role of a few firms in key segments of the financial system is unavoidable. Breaking them up or eliminating all spillover effects is unlikely to be practical or feasible, for reasons discussed elsewhere. If so, regulation could be used to try to counteract the moral hazard problem and reduce the likelihood of their failure. Prudential regulation, such as capital requirements, could be set to hold TBTF firms to higher standards than other financial firms, whether or not those firms are already subject to prudential regulation. This approach would involve a choice between setting a quantitative threshold (based on size, for example) and applying standards to all firms over that size or designating firms believed to systemically important to be subject to the standards on a case-bycase basis.

A framework for prudential regulation is well established in depository banking regulation, featuring the setting of safety and soundness standards and regulatory supervision to ensure adherence to those standards. Historically, banks have been subject to a closer and more intense federal prudential regulatory regime than non-banks because of the systemic risk and moral hazard problems they posed. Some argue that banks generate unique sources of systemic risk (such as deposit taking) that have no analogue in other types of financial firms.[84] If the recent crisis leads to the conclusion that TBTF non-bank financial firms can also be sources of systemic risk and contagion, the same arguments made for regulating banks for systemic risk also apply to TBTF non-banks, however.[85]

There are a wide variety of types of large non-banks, with diverse features. Some non-banks have some of the features that have been viewed as a source of systemic risk, such as leverage and vulnerability to runs, while others do not. There are a few large insurers, which are already regulated for safety and soundness at the state level. On the other hand, state regulators may not be equipped to regulate non-insurance subsidiaries or the overall firm for systemic risk. A study by the Office of Financial Research (OFR) identified several channels through which "asset managers"—a diverse group that includes hedge funds, pension funds, and mutual funds—could pose systemic risks. Others have argued that only activities, not firms, in this industry pose systemic risk. The OFR report identified 10 asset managers each with more than $1 trillion in assets under management.[86]

A "one size fits all" model for regulating firms in different businesses for safety and soundness is unlikely to be practical. Bringing non-banks under the purview of bank regulators raises questions about whether rules designed for banks can be applied to non-banks, and whether the federal bank regulators have the expertise to do so effectively. For example, insurers have argued that bank regulations are not suitable for them and the Fed does not have any specialized expertise in the area of insurance. Another issue is whether to regulate all of the activities of holding companies operating across several lines of business for safety and soundness, or regulate only certain activities that are deemed systemically important, perhaps with legal and financial "firewalls" that isolate the risks of non-regulated activities to the overall holding company.

Regulation cannot prevent all failures from occurring—large, regulated depository institutions failed during the recent financial crisis. Nor is a system without any failures necessarily a desirable one, since risk is inherent in all financial activities. Regulation could aim to prevent large financial firms from taking greater risks than their smaller counterparts because of moral hazard. If successful, fewer failures or episodes involving disruptive losses would occur. If effective, monitoring by regulators might be more economically efficient than monitoring by creditors and counterparties, where a free rider problem reduces the incentive to monitor. In addition, regulators potentially have greater access to relevant information on risk than creditors and counterparties if opacity is a problem with large, complex firms.

This proposal relies on effective regulation by the same regulators who were arguably unable or unwilling to prevent excessive risk taking before and during the crisis by at least a few of the firms that they regulated.[87] Although regulation is intended to limit risky behavior, regulators may inadvertently cause greater correlation of losses across firms by encouraging all firms to engage in similar behavior. Some have argued that large firms are "too complex to regulate," meaning regulators are incapable of identifying or understanding the risks inherent in complicated transactions and corporate structures. For example, the six largest BHCs had more than 1,000 subsidiaries each and the two largest had more than 3,000 each in 2012. Further, their complexity has increased over time—only one BHC had more than 500 subsidiaries in 1990, and the share of assets held outside of depository subsidiaries has grown over time for the largest BHCs.[88] One response to addressing this complexity is to make the regulatory regime more sophisticated, but some critics argue that this approach is likely to backfire.[89] One challenge for the effective regulation of non-banks that are TBTF is that regulators have less experience with business lines other than banking, and thus may initially lack the expertise to regulate them effectively. Others have argued that large firms are "too big to jail," meaning regulators cannot take effective supervisory actions against firms if those actions would undermine the firm's financial health, and thus financial stability.[90]

One way that a regulatory approach could potentially backfire is if a special regulatory regime for TBTF firms is not strict enough, in which case it would exacerbate the moral hazard problem. Critics fear that such a regime would be particularly vulnerable to "regulatory capture," the phenomenon in which the regulated exercise influence over their regulators to ease the burden of regulation. If so, a special regulatory regime could wind up exacerbating the moral hazard problem by, in effect, making TBTF status explicit, signaling to market participants that firms in the special regime enjoyed a protected status and would not be allowed to fail.[91] Instead of increasing the cost of being TBTF, firms in the special regulatory regime could end up borrowing at a lower cost than other firms (since, in effect, these firms would enjoy a lower risk of default).

Many would point to the experience with the GSEs, Fannie Mae and Freddie Mac, before conservatorship as a historical example of how a special regulatory regime could backfire. The GSEs could borrow at a lower cost than other firms because markets believed that the government would not let them fail—they enjoyed even lower borrowing costs than firms that markets might believe were implicitly TBTF but not chartered by the government like the GSEs.[92] Institutional shortcomings, critics argue, led to regulatory capture.[93] The GSEs were subject to their own unique capital requirements, set by statute, under which they were found well capitalized by their regulator at the time, OFHEO, two months before being taken into conservatorship.[94] Yet compared with depositories, GSEs held little capital, were not well diversified, and experienced large losses during the crisis. The worst-case scenario of opponents of a separate regulatory regime for TBTF firms is that such a regime would provide a competitive advantage that would enable more risk taking than before. An example of this scenario was the GSEs' ability to borrow at lower cost than other firms.

Adopting these measures may increase overall costs in the financial system, but in the presence of TBTF, market costs may otherwise be too low from a societal perspective, since risk-taking is too high. For example, requiring loans to be backed with more capital may make lending more expensive and less available, but make the firm less likely to fail. If more capital succeeded in creating a more stable financial system, then the availability of credit could be less volatile over time. At least partly offsetting the higher costs of capital for firms designated as systemically important would be relatively lower costs of capital for other firms.[95]

Even if a heightened prudential regime worked as planned, it could still partly backfire from a systemic risk perspective. To the extent that it causes financial intermediation to migrate away from TBTF firms to firms that are not regulated for safety and soundness, the result could be a less regulated financial system.

Policy Response

Title I of the Dodd-Frank Act created an enhanced prudential regulatory regime for all large bank holding companies and "systemically important" non-bank financial firms. It grants the FSOC the authority to identify systemically important non-bank financial firms (SIFI) by a two-thirds vote, which must be supported by the head of FSOC (the Treasury Secretary). Such a firm would be deemed systemically important on the basis of a council determination that "material financial distress at the [firm] or the nature, scope, size, scale, concentration, interconnectedness, or mix of the activities of the [firm] could pose a threat to the financial stability of the United States." Foreign financial firms operating in the United States could be identified by the council as systemically important. Firms with consolidated assets of less than $50 billion are exempted. Besides the $50 billion threshold, FSOC stated in its final rule that it would consider designating only firms with at least $30 billion in gross notional credit default swaps outstanding in which it was the reference entity, $3.5 billion of derivatives liabilities, $20 billion in debt outstanding, a 15 to 1 leverage ratio (a capital-asset ratio that is not risk-weighted), or a 10% short-term debt ratio.[96]

FSOC has designated three insurers (AIG, Metlife, and Prudential Financial) and one other firm (GE Capital[97]) as systemically important, and therefore subject to heightened prudential regulation.[98] MetLife has requested judicial review of its designation.[99] In April 2015, GE announced that it intended to sell most of GE Capital over the next 18 months to 24 months, in an effort, in part, to no longer be designated as systemically important.[100] FSOC has investigated whether any "asset managers" (a diverse group that includes mutual funds, hedge funds, and private equity funds) are systemically important, but has not made any designations to date.

Under Subtitle C of Title I, the Fed is the prudential regulator for firms that the FSOC has designated as a SIFI and any BHC with total consolidated assets of more than $50 billion. (The FSOC and Fed may raise the asset threshold above $50 billion.) The Fed, with the FSOC's advice, is required to set safety and soundness standards that are more stringent than those applicable to other non-bank financial firms and BHCs that do not pose a systemic risk. At the recommendation of the council or on its own initiative, the Fed may propose additional prudential standards not required by the Dodd-Frank Act or set different standards for different systemically important firms or categories of firms based on various risk-related factors. There are currently about 30 U.S. BHCs with more than $50 billion in consolidated assets.[101] BHCs that participated in the Capital Purchase Program (part of the Troubled Asset Relief Program) would not be able to change their charter to avoid this regulatory regime. Fees are assessed on banks and non-banks regulated under this regime to finance the costs of supervision, as well as the budget of the Office of Financial Research.

The final rule implementing Subtitle C for banks was adopted in February 2014, and banks must be in compliance by January 1, 2015.[102] The final rule includes requirements for stress tests, capital planning, liquidity standards, living wills (discussed in the next section) and risk management. The final rule also requires any bank with more than $50 billion in assets to comply with a 15 to 1 debt to equity limit in the event that the FSOC has determined that it poses a "grave threat" to financial stability. Exposure limits of 25% of a company's capital per single counterparty were included in the proposed rule, but the Fed has indicated that it plans to finalize them at a later date. Enhanced capital requirements have not been required of all BHCs with $50 billion or more in assets.

A large number of foreign banks operating in the United States are also subject to the enhanced prudential regime.[103] Foreign banks operating with more than $50 billion in assets in the United States are required to set up intermediate BHCs that will be subject to heightened standards comparable to those applied to U.S. banks. Less stringent requirements apply to large foreign banks with less than $50 billion in assets in the United States.

In addition, Section 171 of the Dodd-Frank Act (the Collins Amendment) requires the Fed to set capital requirements at the holding company level for non-bank SIFIs and all bank or savings and loan holding companies that are no lower than those applied to banking subsidiaries. For companies with small or no banking subsidiaries, most of the required capital may be based on the activities of and provided by the non-bank subsidiaries. Previously, capital requirements (if there were any) were determined at the subsidiary level by that subsidiary's primary regulator. There are various exceptions to and phase-in periods for this requirement, including an exemption for small holding companies. In the 113th Congress, the Insurance Capital Standards Clarification Act was signed into law (P.L. 113-279), which allows regulators to exempt insurers from the Collins Amendment.

Since 2011, the Financial Stability Board (FSB), an international forum that coordinates the work of national financial authorities and international standard setting bodies, has annually designated "global systemically important banks" (G-SIBs), based on the banks' cross-jurisdictional activity, size, interconnectedness, substitutability, and complexity.[104] The FSB has currently designated 30 banks as G-SIBs, 8 of which are headquartered in the United States. In addition, several of the foreign G-SIBs have U.S. subsidiaries. FSB members have agreed to require the identified firms to meet resolution planning requirements.[105]

In April 2014, the U.S. bank regulators adopted a joint rule that would require these eight banks to meet a supplementary leverage ratio of 5% in order to pay all discretionary bonuses and capital distributions and 6% to be considered well capitalized as of 2018.[106] The supplementary leverage ratio includes off-balance sheet exposures.

In conjunction with the Dodd-Frank Act, Basel III, a nonbinding international agreement on bank regulation that the United States is in the process of implementing,[107] required a common equity surcharge for G-SIBs of at least 1% to "reflect the greater risks that they pose to the financial system."[108] The Fed has proposed a rule implementing this capital surcharge in December 2014.[109] Under its rule, it could designate additional firms as G-SIBs, and it could increase the capital surcharge to as much as 4.5% beginning in 2016. The Fed stated that under its rule, most G-SIBs would face a higher capital surcharge than required by Basel III. Under its proposal, it would currently designate the same eight firms designated by FSB as G-SIBs.

In addition, Basel III creates a counter-cyclical capital buffer that can be modified over the business cycle and a supplementary leverage ratio incorporating off-balance sheet assets, both of which will be applied to only the largest banks (specifically, those subject to the "Advanced Approaches" Rule). In September 2014, the banking regulators finalized a rule implementing Basel III's liquidity coverage ratio, applying it to banks with $250 billion or more in assets or $10 billion or more in on-balance sheet exposure, and a less stringent version of the rule to banks with $50 billion or more in assets. The rule does not apply to non-bank SIFIs, but regulators indicated that non-bank SIFIs would face their own liquidity requirements. The liquidity coverage ratio would require firms to hold enough liquid assets to meet cash flow needs during a stress period.[110]

The FSB has also identified nine insurers as "globally systemically important insurers," three of whom (AIG, Prudential Financial, and MetLife) are headquartered in the United States.[111] FSB members have agreed to require designated insurers to develop recovery and resolution plans and hold more capital than other insurers by 2019. The FSB has released a methodology for identifying global systemically important firms that are not banks or insurers, but has not designated any to date.[112] Some Members of Congress have been concerned that the FSB designation process is superseding the national designation process established by the Dodd-Frank Act.[113]

Minimize Spillover Effects

Options

A criticism of regulation before the crisis was that regulators did not focus enough on how a firm's failure would affect its counterparties or broader financial conditions, or conversely, whether a firm could withstand a crisis situation. Another approach holds that if firms are TBTF because their failure would cause spillover effects that would impair the overall financial system, then instead of altering the TBTF firm, regulators should try to neutralize spillover effects to the point where the failure of a firm would not impair the broader financial system. According to this view, once creditors believed that a firm could now safely be allowed to fail regardless of its size or interconnectedness, the moral hazard problem associated with TBTF would vanish.

One way spillover effects occur is through counterparty risk (the risk of losses because a counterparty in a transaction cannot fulfill its obligations). Examples of how counterparty risk can be reduced include moving transactions to clearinghouses and exchanges, requiring capital/margins for transactions, requiring risk exposures to be hedged, and placing limits on exposure to specific counterparties (transactions, debt, equity holdings, etc.).[114] Adopting these measures may increase overall costs in the financial system. For example, counterparty limits could reduce liquidity and raise costs for transactions that are not standardized enough to be traded on exchanges. In the presence of TBTF, however, market costs may otherwise be too low from a society-wide perspective, because firms lack the proper incentives to monitor or price in counterparty risk.

A drawback to this approach is that spillover effects cannot always be identified beforehand. If counterparty exposure were transparent, in theory all market participants could hedge themselves against failure ahead of time and the failure would not have contagion effects, or at least the government could manage the exposure to prevent contagion. In practice, linkages have proven complex and opaque, and the sources of contagion have proven hard to predict. For example, in September 2008, policy makers reasoned that market participants and policy makers had had several months after the rescue of Bear Stearns to prepare for the failure of Lehman Brothers (indicators such as credit default swaps had signaled an elevated risk of default for months), so allowing it to enter bankruptcy should not be disruptive.[115] Nevertheless, few anticipated that Lehman Brothers' failure would lead to a run on money markets, which proved highly disruptive to commercial paper markets, causing financing problems for many financial and non-financial issuers.

Identifying spillover effects is likely to be more difficult if a firm is not already regulated for safety and soundness. Without a prudential regulator closely monitoring the firm's activities and examining its counterparties, it is less likely that policy makers could quickly and accurately identify who would be exposed to a firm's failure. Much of the necessary information to make that judgment is unlikely to be publicly available.

Another problem is that some solutions shift, rather than eliminate, counterparty risk. For example, moving certain activities onto an exchange or clearinghouse may cause that entity to become "too interconnected to fail."

Policy Response

The Federal Reserve's Regulation F (12 C.F.R., Part 206)—in place before the crisis—limits counterparty exposure for depository institutions. Title I of the Dodd-Frank Act allows the Fed to set exposure limits of 25% of a company's capital per counterparty for firms designated as systemically important by the Financial Stability Oversight Council.[116] To date, a rule implementing this exposure limit has been proposed but not finalized. To reduce counterparty risk, Title VII of the Dodd-Frank Act requires certain swaps, particularly those that involve large financial institutions, to be moved onto clearinghouses or exchanges.[117] Title VIII of the Dodd-Frank Act allows the Financial Stability Oversight Council to identify certain payment, clearing, and settlement systems and activities as systemically important "financial market utilities," and allows the Federal Reserve, Securities and Exchange Commission, or Commodity and Futures Trading Commission to regulate those systems and activities for enhanced prudential supervision. It also allows systemically important systems to borrow from the Fed in "unusual or exigent circumstances." In 2012, regulators issued a final rule implementing Title VIII and designated eight financial market utilities, including major clearinghouses, as systemically important.[118]

Resolving a Large, Interconnected Failing Firm

Options

Prior to the financial crisis, failing banks were resolved through the FDIC's resolution regime, while certain other financial firms, such as broker-dealers, were resolved through the corporate bankruptcy system.[119] Bankruptcy is a judicial process initiated by creditors in order to recover debts and other liabilities, while the FDIC's resolution regime is an administrative process initiated by the FDIC. Examples of the types of powers that the FDIC can exercise to resolve a depository include transferring and freezing assets, paying obligations, repudiating contracts, and obtaining judicial stays.[120]

The FDIC typically resolves failed banks through the "purchase and assumption" method, under which the bank is closed and some or all of the assets and deposits of the failed bank are sold to healthy banks.[121] If losses are too large to be absorbed by creditors, they are absorbed by the FDIC's deposit insurance fund, which is pre-funded through assessments on depositories. The purchase and assumption method avoids open-ended government assistance and keeps the FDIC out of the business of running banks, but an unintended consequence is that it encourages greater concentration, since the only entity capable of absorbing a large failed bank is likely to be an even larger institution.

One rationale behind a resolution regime for banks is that the need to safeguard federally insured deposits (which can be withdrawn rapidly) requires a swift resolution and gives the FDIC, which insures the deposits, priority over other creditors. Prompt corrective action and least cost resolution requirements are intended to minimize losses to the FDIC. The FDIC may initiate a resolution before failure has occurred—thereby limiting losses to the FDIC and other creditors— whereas a bankruptcy process cannot be initiated by creditors until default has occurred.

Another example of a resolution regime is the one applied to Fannie Mae and Freddie Mac. Their regulator, the Federal Housing Finance Agency (FHFA), assumed control of Fannie Mae and Freddie Mac in September 2008 when FHFA determined that they were critically undercapitalized. Since then, Fannie Mae and Freddie Mac have operated under government conservatorship.[122]

Part of what makes some financial firms too big to fail is the nature of the bankruptcy process, according to some analysts. A firm that dominates important financial market segments cannot be liquidated without disrupting the availability of credit, it is argued. They argue that the deliberate pace of the bankruptcy process is not equipped to avoid the runs and contagion inherent in the failure of a financial firm, and that the effects on systemic risk are not taken into account when decisions are made in the bankruptcy process. The bankruptcy experience of Lehman Brothers is viewed as evidence of why the current bankruptcy process cannot be successful for a TBTF firm.

Proponents argue that a resolution regime for all TBTF financial firms, regardless of whether the firm is a depository, offers an alternative to propping up failing firms with government assistance (as was the case with Bear Stearns and AIG in 2008) or suffering the systemic consequences of a protracted and messy bankruptcy (as was the case with Lehman Brothers).[123] In principle, a TBTF resolution regime could include a receivership process (where the government seizes control of the firm in order to wind it down), a conservatorship process (where the government seizes control in order to continue operations), or both. The FDIC's typical treatment of a failed bank is an example of a receivership process; FHFA's treatment of Fannie Mae and Freddie Mac since 2008 is an example of the conservatorship process.[124] Often, banks in receivership are resolved through acquisitions by healthy firms. In the case of a large firm, acquisitions would result in the acquiring firm becoming even larger. Were one of the nation's very largest firms to fail, it is not clear what firm would have the capacity to acquire it, in which case some other method of resolution would be necessary.

Supporting the argument for a special resolution regime, the failures of large depositories during the crisis that were subject to the FDIC's resolution regime, such as Wachovia and Washington Mutual, were less disruptive to the financial system than the failure of Lehman Brothers, even though Wachovia and Lehman Brothers were sequential (46th and 47th largest, respectively) on *Fortune*'s list of the 500 largest companies of 2007.[125] (Wells Fargo acquired Wachovia before the FDIC formally became receiver.) Whether the resolution of a non-bank could be handled as smoothly as these two banks is an open question.[126]

Critics argue that a resolution regime, depending on its design, could give policy makers too much discretionary power, which could result in higher costs to the government and preferential treatment of favored creditors during the resolution. In other words, it could enable "backdoor bailouts" that could allow government assistance to be funneled to the firm or its creditors beyond what would be available in bankruptcy, perpetuating the moral hazard problem.[127] The normal FDIC resolution regime minimizes the potential for these problems through its statutory requirements of least cost resolution and prompt corrective action. It would be expected that a resolution regime for

TBTF firms, by contrast, would at times be required to subordinate a least cost principle to systemic risk considerations, which the FDIC regime permits. Therefore, a resolution could be more costly to the government than the bankruptcy process. (On the other hand, an administrative resolution process could potentially avoid some of the costs of bankruptcy, such as some legal fees and runs by creditors that further undermine the firm's finances.) Critics also point to the conservatorship of Fannie Mae and Freddie Mac—who have received government support on an ongoing basis since 2008—as evidence that a resolution regime could turn out to be too open ended and be used to prop up TBTF firms as ongoing entities, competing with private sector rivals on an advantageous basis because of direct government subsidies. The Housing and Economic Recovery Act (HERA; P.L. 110-289) required mandatory receivership for the GSEs if they became insolvent, but quarterly transfers from Treasury prevented insolvency. As noted above, uncertainty before the fact about which firms are TBTF may lead policy makers to err on the side of taking more failing firms than necessary into the special resolution process instead of allowing them to enter bankruptcy.

If policy makers, wary of the turmoil caused by Lehman Brothers' failure, were unwilling to pursue the bankruptcy option in the future, opposing a resolution regime may be tantamount to tacitly accepting future "bailouts," unless some other policy change is made that future policy makers view as a workable alternative. As an alternative to a special resolution regime, some critics call for amending the bankruptcy code to create a special chapter for complex financial firms to address problems that have been identified, such as a speedier process and the ability to reorganize.[128] This approach was pursued in H.R. 5421, which passed the House in the 113th Congress. To some extent, these concerns are already addressed in the bankruptcy code. For example, the bankruptcy process already allows qualified financial contracts to be netted out. In the case of Lehman Brothers, healthy business units were sold to competitors relatively quickly through the bankruptcy process, and remain in operation today.

Until a TBTF firm fails, it is open to debate whether a special resolution regime could successfully achieve what it is intended to do—shut down a failing firm without triggering systemic disruption. One key challenge that has been identified is the resolution of foreign subsidiaries.[129] Given the size of the firms involved and the unanticipated transmission of systemic risk, it remains to be seen whether the government could impose losses on any creditors without triggering contagion—or would be willing to try. A receiver would face the same short-term incentives to limit losses to creditors to limit systemic risk that caused policy makers to rescue firms in the recent crisis in order to restore stability. If the receiver is guided by those short-term incentives, the only difference between a resolution regime and a "bailout" might turn out to be that shareholder equity is wiped out, at presumably relatively little savings to the government.

Policy Response

In July 2008, Congress enacted HERA, which included provisions creating a new regulator (the Federal Housing Finance Agency or FHFA) for the housing GSEs (the Federal Home Loan Banks, Fannie Mae, and Freddie Mac). The FHFA was given augmented powers to resolve the GSEs.[130] Under these powers, FHFA can manage assets, sign contracts, terminate claims, collect obligations, and perform management functions. In September 2008, Fannie Mae and Freddie Mac entered FHFA conservatorship, upon which FHFA took control of their operations while maintaining them as ongoing enterprises.[131] HERA also gave the Treasury Secretary unlimited authority to lend or invest in the GSEs through the end of 2009. This authority has been used to cover the GSEs' losses and prevent insolvency during conservatorship, and funds from Treasury continued to be transferred until 2012. While existing shareholders saw their equity value plummet at the time of conservatorship, creditors and other counterparties have continued to be paid in full.

Title I of the Dodd-Frank Act requires systemically important firms (SIFIs) and BHCs with at least $50 billion in consolidated assets to periodically prepare resolution plans, also called "living wills," explaining how they could be resolved in a rapid and orderly manner. Failure to submit a credible resolution plan would trigger regulatory action. Title I also creates early remediation requirements for non-bank SIFIs that are in financial distress (banks already had early remediation requirements under existing statute).

Title II of the Dodd-Frank Act creates a resolution regime for any financial firm whose failure would have "serious adverse effects on financial stability." (The firm does not have to have been previously subject to enhanced prudential regulation under Title I to be resolved under Title II.) However, subsidiaries that are insurance companies would be resolved under state law, certain broker-dealers would be resolved by the Securities Investor Protection Corporation, and insured depository subsidiaries would be resolved under the FDIC's traditional resolution regime. The process for taking a firm into resolution has multiple steps and actors. First, a group of regulators (the group varies depending on the type of firm, but must always include the approval of two-thirds of the Federal Reserve's Board of Governors) must make a written recommendation to the Treasury Secretary that a firm should be resolved, explaining why bankruptcy would be inappropriate. Second, the Treasury Secretary must determine that resolution is necessary to avoid a default that would pose systemic risk to the financial system, and default cannot be prevented through a private sector alternative. Prior identification by the FSOC could be used as evidence that the firm's failure poses systemic risk, but it is not a necessary condition. Third, if the company disputes the Treasury Secretary's findings, it has limited rights to appeal in federal court. Finally, the FDIC manages the resolution.

The Dodd-Frank Act provides the FDIC with receivership powers, modeled on its bank receivership powers, with some differences, such as requirements that the FDIC consult with the primary regulator. As receiver, the FDIC can manage assets, sign contracts, terminate claims, collect obligations, and perform management functions. The Dodd-Frank Act sets priorities among classes of unsecured creditors, with senior executives and directors coming last before shareholders in order of priority. It requires that similarly situated creditors be treated similarly, unless doing so would increase the cost to the government. The FDIC is allowed to create bridge companies, as a way to divide good and bad assets, for a limited period of time to facilitate the resolution. Unlike FHFA's resolution regime, the Dodd-Frank regime does not allow for conservatorship.

The Dodd-Frank Act calls for shareholders and creditors to bear losses and management "responsible for the condition of the company" to be removed. The FDIC is allowed to use its funds to provide credit to the firm while in receivership if funding cannot be obtained from private credit markets. Unlike the resolution regime for banks, there is no least cost resolution requirement and the regime is not pre-funded (the FDIC may borrow from Treasury to finance it). Instead, costs that cannot be recouped in the process of resolution must be made up after the fact through assessments on counterparties (to the extent that their losses were smaller under receivership than they would have been in a traditional bankruptcy process) and risk-based assessments on financial firms with assets exceeding $50 billion. Since the rationale for limiting losses to counterparties is to prevent systemic risk, it is unclear how those counterparties could be assessed after the fact without also posing some systemic risk. A lack of pre-funding means that a firm's resolution will, in effect, be financed by its competitors (i.e., firms with assets exceeding $50 billion) instead of itself. The FDIC is limited to providing assistance in the resolution up to 10% of the failed firm's total consolidated assets in the first 30 days of the resolution; thereafter the limit becomes 90% of total consolidated assets available for repayment.

The FDIC has stated,

> the most promising resolution strategy [under Title II] from our point view will be to place the parent company into receivership and to pass its assets, principally investments in its subsidiaries, to a newly created bridge holding company. This will allow subsidiaries that are equity solvent and contribute to the franchise value of the firm to remain open and avoid the disruption that would likely accompany their closings....
>
> Equity claims of the firm's shareholders and the claims of the subordinated and unsecured debt holders will be left behind in the receivership....
>
> Therefore, initially, the bridge holding company will be owned by the receivership. The next stage in the resolution is to transfer ownership and control of the surviving franchise to private hands....
>
> The second step will be the conversion of the debt holders' claims to equity. The old debt holders of the failed parent will become the owners of the new company.... [132]

This approach has been dubbed "Single Point of Entry," and the FDIC proposed a rule implementing it in December 2013.[133] A *BGOV* study argues that Single Point of Entry will only mitigate moral hazard if the holding company holds sufficient common equity and debt that can absorb losses in resolution at the parent level; otherwise, investors will anticipate that public funds will be used to absorb losses.[134] Financial regulators have indicated that they plan to propose a rule requiring long-term debt at the holding company level.[135]

SELECTED LEGISLATION IN THE 114TH CONGRESS

S. 1484, as reported by the Senate Banking Committee on June 2, 2015, would increase the $50 billion asset threshold to $500 billion for enhanced regulation under Title I of the Dodd-Frank Act. Similar to the existing non-bank designation process, banks with assets between $50 billion and $500 billion would be subject to enhanced regulation if FSOC designated them (by two-thirds vote, including the chair) as systemically important following a referral by the Fed.

Compared with the current non-bank designation process, S. 1484 would require FSOC to provide more information to (bank or non-bank) institutions and give them more opportunities to take actions to avoid or reverse SIFI designation. It would increase public disclosure requirements surrounding the designation process. S. 1484 would also require GAO to conduct a study of the Fed's enhanced regulatory regime for banks and non-banks and require the Fed to report to Congress at least every two years on its supervision of non-bank SIFIs. S. 1484 would also exempt banks with under $10 billion in assets from the Volcker Rule. The bill also adjusts all of these thresholds for future GDP growth.

S.Con.Res. 11, the FY2016 budget resolution, was agreed to in the House on April 30, 2015, and the Senate on May 5, 2015. It creates a nonbinding deficit-neutral budget reserve fund that allows for future legislation "relating to any bank holding companies with over $500 billion in total assets to better protect taxpayers, including such measures as capital or leverage requirements, restrictions on the growth, activities, or operations of a company, or divestiture of assets or operations of any company that is unable to present a credible plan to facilitate an orderly bankruptcy or resolution."

CONCLUSION

Contagion stemming from problems at TBTF (or too interconnected to fail) firms is widely regarded to have been one of the primary sources of systemic risk during the acute phase of the recent financial crisis. To avoid contagion, a series of ad hoc government interventions were undertaken that protected creditors and counterparties—and in a few cases, also managers and shareholders—of large and interconnected firms from losses. Economic theory suggests that these interventions exacerbated the moral hazard implications of TBTF, reducing the incentive for creditors and counterparties to safeguard against extreme outcomes, and increased the incentive to become larger and more interconnected going forward. Competing theories blame the lack of regulatory authority and failed regulation for the role of TBTF in the recent crisis. The failures of both highly regulated banks and lightly regulated non-banks suggest that neither lack of regulation nor failed regulation were solely responsible for TBTF.

Policy before the financial crisis could be characterized as an implicit market discipline approach with ambiguity about which firms policymakers considered to be TBTF and how the imminent failure of a systemically important firm might be addressed. This ambiguity was defended on the grounds that it would result in less moral hazard than if TBTF firms were explicitly identified, since the ambiguity would promote market discipline. As the crisis unfolded, policy quickly shifted to an expectation of government assistance, where Bear Stearns, Fannie Mae, Freddie Mac, and AIG received direct government support and several emergency programs were instituted to ensure that other financial firms remained liquid and solvent. Not every large failing firm received assistance, however, with Lehman Brothers being the notable exception. Both before and during the crisis, policy could be characterized as ad hoc because arguably no general approach or principles were articulated that clearly signaled to firms or investors how a systemically important firm could expect to be treated in different scenarios. Some believe that this policy uncertainty made the crisis worse.

The rapid shift from market discipline to government assistance during the crisis undermines the future credibility of the pre-crisis policy approach. If policy makers wanted to return to a market discipline approach, making that approach effective would arguably require statutory changes that bolster policy makers' credibility by "tying their hands" to make assistance more difficult in the event of a future TBTF failure. This could be accomplished by eliminating broad, open-ended authority that was invoked during the last crisis, such as Section 13(3) of the Federal Reserve Act and the FDIC's systemic risk exception to least cost resolution. Policy makers cannot be prevented from enacting future legislation allowing assistance, however, much as TARP was enacted expeditiously when the crisis worsened in September 2008. If investors do not believe that market discipline will be maintained because policy makers face short-term incentives to provide government assistance in times of crisis, then a "no bailouts" promise would not prevent moral hazard.

One view is that the genie cannot be put back in the bottle—market participants now believe that the government will provide assistance to TBTF firms based on the 2008 experience, in which case they face little incentive to monitor or respond to excessive risk taking. If so, the policy options to mitigate moral hazard are to regulate TBTF firms for safety and soundness or use government policy to reduce the systemic risk posed by TBTF firms.

In theory, a special regulatory regime for TBTF firms could set safety and soundness standards at a strict enough level to neutralize moral hazard effects.

The complexity and interconnectedness of large firms complicates their effective regulation, however. Moreover, a special regulatory regime for TBTF firms could backfire if regulatory capture occurs. Special regulation makes explicit which firms are TBTF, removing any ambiguity that might promote market discipline. As market discipline wanes, the burden on regulators to mitigate moral hazard increases. If regulators are unwilling or unable to apply regulatory standards that negate the benefits of being TBTF, then being subject to the special regulatory regime could give TBTF firms a competitive advantage over their industry rivals. The experience of Fannie Mae and Freddie Mac points to the dangers of this approach. Those two firms were subject to their own regulatory regime prior to the crisis and were able to borrow at lower interest rates than other financial firms, presumably because of the implicit government guarantee of their obligations.

Systemic risk stemming from TBTF can also be mitigated by reducing potential spillover and contagion effects. Examples of proposals to reduce contagion effects include a special resolution regime for failing systemically important firms and placing limits on counterparty exposure to large firms. Events in 2008, however, demonstrate the challenge in eliminating systemic risk posed by TBTF firms because it is unlikely that policy makers will correctly anticipate all of the channels of contagion in a crisis. Moreover, in determining whether to use government resources to limit losses to creditors, the receiver faces the same short-term incentives to spare creditors from losses that lead to moral hazard. Critics point to the open-ended assistance to Fannie Mae and Freddie Mac since 2008 as a cautionary tale, although this was through government conservatorship, rather than receivership.

Some argue for eliminating TBTF directly by reducing the size or scope of the largest firms. It is uncertain what size limit would eliminate TBTF—given that interconnectedness is a nebulous concept—and policymakers would only know if they had set the right size limit by observing what occurs after a firm fails. Weighed against the benefits of eliminating the TBTF problem, the benefits to the financial system that would be lost by eliminating large firms are also disputed. In the case of reducing scope, some large firms would remain, and they would be less diversified against risk. Fannie Mae and Freddie Mac are examples of large, narrowly focused firms that many nonetheless viewed as TBTF.

A comprehensive policy is likely to incorporate more than one approach because different approaches are aimed at different parts of the problem. Some approaches focus on preventive measures (keeping TBTF firms out of trouble), whereas others are reactive (addressing what to do in the event of a

TBTF failure). Some policy approaches are complementary—others could undermine each other. A market discipline approach is arguably most likely to succeed if coupled with size limits—although size limits thwart market-based profit incentives and outcomes. Policies that involve identification of TBTF firms, such as a special regulatory regime, are less compatible with a market discipline approach. Efforts to minimize spillover effects could be more effective if the TBTF firms are regulated for safety and soundness, so that spillover effects can more easily be identified ahead of time. Policy makers have historically coped with the moral hazard associated with deposit insurance through a combination of safety and soundness regulation, a resolution regime, and limits on spillover effects (e.g., limits on counterparty exposure). (Market discipline's role is limited by deposit insurance, but it plays a role with uninsured depositors and other creditors.) Yet TBTF poses some additional challenges to the bank regulation model, such as the difficulties of imposing a strict least cost resolution requirement on a resolution regime and effectively regulating firms with complex and wide-ranging activities.

Each of these policy approaches to coping with TBTF has strengths and weaknesses; there is no silver-bullet solution to the problem because future policy makers face incentives to deviate from the approach to avoid crises, please interest groups, increase financial innovation and the availability of credit, and so on. Judging the relative merits of each policy approach depends in part on which approach future policy makers can best commit to and effectively carry out.

The Dodd-Frank Act devised a strategy to end TBTF that, to varying degrees, incorporated each approach discussed in this report. Only one of the approaches outlined above has the primary goal of reducing the size of large firms, and the Dodd-Frank Act's policy changes were limited in this area. Some take the fact that the largest financial firms have generally become larger since the crisis (at least in dollar terms) as a sign that the TBTF problem has not been solved. In principle, the TBTF problem can be eliminated even if large firms do not shrink, but it is difficult to verify success because ultimately, the only definitive test of whether the strategy succeeds is whether the failure of a large firm can be managed without a "bailout" and whether large firms stay healthy in a financial downturn—events that may not occur for years or even decades. Until then, perceptions of whether the TBTF problem still exists may develop (and be observable in market data), which could subsequently be proven true or false.

Although TBTF was one cause of systemic risk in the recent crisis, it was not the only one. The Dodd-Frank Act also attempted to address other sources of systemic risk. Although the broader issue of systemic risk is beyond the scope of this report, some policy options discussed in this report may be more effective at mitigating systemic risk if applied more broadly than to TBTF firms exclusively. Otherwise, some sources of systemic risk may migrate to firms not regulated for safety and soundness, without increasing the stability of the overall financial system. If systemic risk mainly stems from certain activities, regardless of size, a policy focus on large institutions could risk creating a false sense of security.

Risk is central to financial activity, so an optimal system is probably not one where large firms never fail. An optimal system is one in which a large firm can fail without destabilizing the financial system. The only system that can guarantee that large firms will not cause systemic risk is one without large firms, but a system without large firms may be less efficient. Other approaches seek to limit systemic risk to acceptable levels. Creating a more stable financial system by mitigating the moral hazard associated with TBTF may result in credit becoming more expensive and less available in the short run, but the availability of credit could be less volatile over time. At least partly offsetting the higher costs of capital for firms designated as systemically important would be relatively lower costs of capital for other firms. Some policy makers would consider a tradeoff of less credit for a more stable financial system to be a tradeoff worth taking, considering that the recent crisis resulted in the deepest and longest recession since the Great Depression. Arguably, part of the cause of the crisis was that credit became too readily available, at least in some sectors (e.g., the housing bubble).

APPENDIX. SELECTED HISTORICAL EXPERIENCES WITH "TOO BIG TO FAIL"

Before the Recent Crisis

There have always been large financial firms in the United States, but concentration within the banking sector and non-bank financial sector has increased in recent decades. This growth is a reflection of both policy changes that made growth easier and market changes that made growth more profitable. For example, technological change altered the types of financial products that could be offered and the relative costs of offering them, and investments in information technology may be subject to economies of scale.

Two important policy changes that allowed financial firms to become larger since the Great Depression were the erosion of the separation of banking from other financial services (such as investment banking) and the erosion of prohibitions on interstate banking.

The Glass-Steagall Act forbade commercial banks from underwriting or trading in certain types of securities and affiliating with a business engaged principally in investment banking. It forbade investment banks from accepting deposits and forbade the same company from owning a commercial bank and an investment bank. The Bank Holding Company Act prohibited banks from affiliating with companies engaging in insurance underwriting and defined the activities closely related to banking that banks were allowed to engage in.[136] Implementation of these restrictions relied upon regulators' judgment and interpretation, which evolved over time. Regulators interpreted which securities commercial banks were eligible to purchase, which activities fell within the "business of banking," and how closely affiliated commercial banks could be with investment banks. From the 1970s on, regulators began to interpret Glass-Steagall more loosely, and differences between commercial banks and investment banks began to erode.[137]

The Gramm-Leach-Bliley Act (GLBA) of 1999 repealed the prohibition on affiliations between commercial banks and investment banks or insurance companies, and created a financial holding company (FHC) structure to facilitate those affiliations. Within a FHC or BHC, firewalls are required to prevent financial problems at non-depository subsidiary from affecting a depository subsidiary. (GLBA kept intact the provisions of Glass-Steagall preventing investment banks from accepting deposits.) While GLBA made it easier for firms in diverse lines of business to operate under a holding company structure, it also formalized Federal Reserve supervision and regulation of complex financial firms. GLBA formalized the Fed's role as "umbrella regulator" of BHCs and financial holding companies and the Office of Thrift Supervision as umbrella regulator of thrift holding companies, and allowed the regulators to set consolidated capital standards at the holding company level. The Fed's role as umbrella regulator gave it very limited powers, however, to regulate or examine subsidiaries that already had a functional regulator, such as investment firms and insurers.[138]

Traditionally, banks were chartered to operate in one state. Interstate banking by national banks was allowed with a state's consent under the McFadden Act of 1927 (P.L. 69-639). The absence of state consent prevented widespread interstate banking for the next several decades, curbing the growth in nationwide banks. A series of legislative and regulatory changes led to the spread of interstate banking in the 1980s and 1990s. The Riegle-Neal Interstate Banking and Branching Efficiency Act of 1994 (P.L. 103-328) further liberalized interstate banking.[139] The Riegle-Neal Act prevented mergers resulting in a BHC exceeding 10% of national deposits and 30% of a state's deposits.

The history of government bailouts on TBTF grounds before 2008 is largely limited to the cases of a few banks. In cases where government intervention to prevent the failure of non-banks on TBTF grounds was urged (Long-Term Capital Management), the government ultimately decided not to intervene financially to save the companies, and the spillover effects were limited. The **Appendix** does not review cases where federal assistance was provided on other than systemic risk grounds. Most of the economic arguments of how financial firms are prone to contagion and runs do not apply to non-financial firms. Examples include assistance to non-financial firms such as Lockheed in 1970, Chrysler in 1980, and Chrysler and GM in 2008, where assistance was justified on the grounds of avoiding negative effects on the region or industry.[140]

Resolution of Banks Before and After the Federal Deposit Insurance Corporation Improvement Act

Currently, the two main methods for resolving failed banks are "depositor payoff" (winding down the bank and paying off depositors) and "purchase and assumption" (selling parts of failed banks, such as deposits and sound assets, to healthy banks).[141] In either method, uninsured depositors and creditors are compensated according to the priority of their claims to the extent that the proceeds of the sale or liquidation allow; only insured depositors are guaranteed to be fully compensated. In practice, it was standard for the acquiring bank to take on the accounts of the uninsured depositors in the case of a purchase and assumption, resulting in no losses for the latter.[142] According to Stern and Feldman, "Reliance on [purchase and assumption] led the deposit insurer to cover all depositors. The FDIC covered more than 99 percent of uninsured depositors from 1985 to 1991, a period in which roughly 1,200 commercial banks failed."[143]

In the past, an alternative option for resolving troubled banks was open bank assistance. Under open bank assistance, the FDIC could make loans to banks that could no longer obtain funding from the private sector in order to keep banks operating as an ongoing concern as an alternative to resolving them. Banks receiving open bank assistance were often required by the FDIC to replace management and dilute shareholders, but creditors and depositors would be unaffected. In 1950, Congress granted the FDIC the ability to give open bank assistance to troubled banks if the bank's "continued existence was determined to be 'essential' to providing adequate banking services in the community," leaving the determination of "essential" to the FDIC.[144] "Essentiality" was invoked 10 times between 1971 and 1991, the largest example of which was for Continental Illinois, which is discussed below in detail.[145] In 1982, the Garn-St. Germain Act broadened the FDIC's ability to provide open bank assistance to include cases where the FDIC determined that it would cost less than liquidation.

Open bank assistance was not used until the 1970s, and was not used frequently until the Savings and Loan Crisis in the 1980s. Between 1980 and 1992, it was used for 133 banks, which were larger on average than banks resolved under the other methods. 70 of the 133 instances were for banks within two specific BHCs, BancTexas and First City Bancorporation of Texas. While these two were not among the largest banks in the country, the FDIC provided them with open bank assistance on the grounds that their failure would lead to contagion throughout Texas banks, which had been weakened by the energy bust.[146]

Open bank assistance could be used because a bank was deemed TBTF, but it could also be used for other reasons, including regional difficulties, which were more acute before interstate banking. Some of the banks to which it was applied were large by state standards, but were not particularly large at a national level (which few banks were, at the time). Furthermore, prior to various legislation in the 1980s, the purchase and assumption method was relatively more costly and often resulted in litigation, making open bank assistance relatively more attractive from regulators' perspective. Thus, it is difficult to establish how many of these 133 cases were motivated by TBTF concerns, or how much this experience had led banks, creditors, and counterparties to conclude that large banks would not be allowed to fail.

Regulators could also avoid resolving a bank through regulatory forbearance. An example of regulatory forbearance is allowing banks to temporarily operate with capital below required levels. Regulators could choose to allow regulatory forbearance on TBTF grounds, although in practice, it often occurred with small thrifts in the 1980s.[147]

Many economists criticized the handling of bank resolutions in the 1980s, arguing that regulatory forbearance worsened the moral hazard problem, because a troubled bank allowed to remain in operation had even more incentive to take risks. Legislation in 1991 reduced the potential for regulatory forbearance by requiring prompt corrective action and least cost resolution of troubled banks.[148] These legislative changes and others made open bank assistance less likely, and according to FDIC data, open bank assistance was not used between 1993 and 2008.[149] (Purchase and assumption continued to be the main method of resolution after 1991, but bids involving only insured deposits became more common.) Current law, as amended by the 1991 legislation, allows the FDIC to waive the least cost resolution method if the Treasury Secretary (in consultation with the President, Federal Reserve, and FDIC) believes that least cost resolution would cause systemic risk, however.[150] TBTF is potential grounds for invoking this systemic risk exception. Thus, while the 1991 legislation is perceived to have reduced moral hazard at small banks, it is not clear whether it had a significant effect on the TBTF problem.

Penn Central Railroad

After unsuccessfully seeking financial assistance from Congress and the Fed, Penn Central Railroad filed for bankruptcy in June 1970. At that time, it had $82 million in commercial paper outstanding, and when it filed for bankruptcy, the Fed feared its bankruptcy would cause disruption in the commercial paper market for all borrowers. The Fed temporarily removed legal interest rate ceilings to avoid a credit crunch and "made clear that the Federal Reserve discount window would be available to assist banks in meeting the needs of businesses unable to roll over maturing commercial paper."[151] In other words, the Fed was willing to assist the counterparties to prevent contagion from a perceived TBTF failure, rather than preventing the firm from failing. In any case, the perceived contagion from that source did not materialize—data do not indicate an unusual amount of discount window lending by the Fed in 1970.[152]

Beginning in 1974, the federal government provided financial assistance to maintain the viability of passenger rail service in the wake of Penn Central's bankruptcy. This assistance was not provided to prevent bankruptcy or to maintain financial stability, and is therefore beyond the scope of this report.

Franklin National

Franklin National, the nation's 20th-largest bank, experienced financial difficulties in 1974. Fearing that its failure would destabilize money markets, the Fed purchased its foreign exchange balances and futures contracts and provided it loans through the discount window to keep it afloat. When

Franklin was resolved later that year, the FDIC assumed Franklin's $1.7 billion unpaid discount window loan.[153]

Continental Illinois

Continental Illinois was the nation's seventh-largest bank in 1984.[154] Continental Illinois losses have been tied to its aggressive growth in commercial lending beginning in the late 1970s.[155] Continental Illinois' problems began in 1982 with the failure of a correspondent bank, and came to a head in 1984 with a run by some uninsured depositors. Despite being subject to the FDIC's resolution regime, the Comptroller of the Currency at the time testified that Continental Illinois could not be allowed to fail because it would have caused the failure of more than 100 banks with deposits at Continental Illinois, and dozens of corporate customers.[156] It began receiving federal assistance in 1984 in the form of discount window loans from the Fed that peaked at $8 billion and a guarantee by the FDIC of all uninsured depositors and creditors. Eventually, policy makers decided a more permanent solution was needed. Instead of taking Continental Illinois into receivership, the FDIC purchased $3.5 billion of problem loans and $1 billion of preferred shares, and repaid $3.5 billion in loans from the Federal Reserve. The final cost to FDIC was $1.1 billion.[157] The chairman of the board and chief executive officer were replaced, and the FDIC received an option to acquire Continental Illinois' stock to cover potential losses.

Continental Illinois was regulated for safety and soundness, operating in an era before many financial regulations were liberalized by the Gramm-Leach-Bliley Act and other legislative and regulatory changes.[158] One problem identified was the pace with which regulators addressed Continental's problems—the bank failed in September; the previous May, OCC had stated that the bank's capital ratios "compared favorably to those of other multinational banks."[159] Had regulators addressed Continental Illinois' financial problems sooner, the ultimate cost to taxpayers may have been lower. Continental Illinois also led to a more explicit TBTF policy, at least for banks. At a congressional hearing, Comptroller of the Currency Todd Conover testified that "the federal government won't currently allow any of the nation's 11 largest banks to fail," but did not name those banks.[160] One study found that after this testimony, the 11 largest banks received higher ratings on their bonds and borrowed at lower costs.[161]

Long-Term Capital Management

In 1998, the hedge fund Long-Term Capital Management (LTCM) experienced a liquidity crisis as a result of large leveraged trading losses resulting from an unanticipated widening of credit spreads. To avoid a failure that the Fed thought could be destabilizing to the financial system as a whole, the New York Fed organized a group of large financial institutions to offer LTCM private assistance in the form of a $3.6 billion capital injection, without the use of any public funds or guarantees. The Fed was concerned that liquidating LTCM's large trading positions could destabilize financial markets and impose large losses on counterparties. In the weeks before the capital injection, LTCM's capital had been rapidly depleted by losses, but its net asset value was still positive, albeit small, at the time of the intervention.[162] The Fed's actions in this case could be described as helping the rescuing firms (who were also LTCM counterparties) to overcome the collective action problem—the firms involved were better off recapitalizing the firm than liquidating it, but unless they could act collectively, it was in no firm's individual interest to recapitalize it alone. Critics claimed the Fed's intervention was unnecessary, as an alternative offer from another group of investors to purchase the firm on less attractive terms was also made.[163]

As in 2007, overall markets came under unusual stress and became illiquid in 1998. Unlike 2007, the stress passed and markets recovered quickly in 1998. Although it is unknown what would have happened had LTCM been allowed to fail, this experience seemed at the time to provide a framework for coping with problems at a TBTF firm—preventing LTCM's failure prevented contagion from spreading to other institutions or markets, and conditions were able to quickly normalize. Since the government did not offer financial assistance, it could continue to claim that TBTF firms would not be bailed out. LTCM's problems did not cause investors to doubt the health of similar firms, as happened in the recent crisis. A lesson that many drew from this episode was that market mechanisms and existing policy tools could contain the contagion effects resulting from liquidity problems at a highly leveraged and interconnected firm that was not regulated for safety and soundness.

Firms in 2008

Several large firms experienced difficulty in 2008, and these problems were resolved in a number of ways. Bear Stearns and AIG were rescued from failure through government assistance. Lehman Brothers filed for bankruptcy.

Fannie Mae and Freddie Mac entered government conservatorship. Wachovia and Washington Mutual were acquired by other banks without government assistance.

As the name implies, "too big to fail" requires both size and the prospect of failure. Part of the reason the policy issue came to the forefront in 2008 and not earlier is because the crisis led to so many failures of large and small firms. The probability of a large (or small) firm failing in 2008 was much higher than in the decades of financial stability leading up to 2008. More contentious is the argument made by some that the probability of failure was also higher in 2008 because large firms were taking greater risks than in previous decades. Evidence presented in support of this argument includes the rise over time in financial firms' use of leverage (debt-to-equity ratios),[164] unstable sources of liquidity, and complex financial instruments such as credit default swaps (which could be used by a firm to reduce or increase certain forms of risk).

Bear Stearns

In the recent crisis, the investment bank Bear Stearns was the first TBTF firm to receive government assistance to avert failure.[165] Bear Stearns was not a BHC regulated for safety and soundness, nor subject to the FDIC's resolution regime.[166] It came under severe liquidity pressures in early March 2008, when creditors refused to roll over short-term debt and counterparties withdrew funds, in what observers have coined a non-bank run. An SEC press release a few days before its takeover indicated that Bear Stearns had $17 billion of cash and other liquid assets—an amount that was quickly depleted by the run.[167] The run was set off by concerns that Bear Stearns held a large portfolio of illiquid, "troubled" assets that investors believed would continue losing value in the future and deplete its remaining capital.

By the weekend of March 15, it had become clear that Bear Stearns could not survive the run by creditors. Although Bear Stearns was not indisputably "too big to fail" (it was the 138th-largest firm by revenues in 2007 on *Fortune Magazine*'s Fortune 500 list),[168] some policy makers argued for government intervention on the grounds that Bear Stearns was "too interconnected to fail," meaning too many counterparties and markets would be disrupted by a traditional bankruptcy filing.[169] The Fed sought a healthy firm to acquire Bear Stearns, but was unable to find a willing partner without financial assistance. Over the weekend of March 15, the Fed arranged and assisted in the takeover of Bear Stearns by J.P. Morgan Chase at a very low purchase price (originally $2 per share, subsequently increased to $10 per share), which Bear Stearns' board of directors agreed to accept instead of pursuing a bankruptcy filing.

The takeover led to replacement of some of Bear Stearns' management and the low share price meant that shareholders were effectively diluted, although they likely fared better than they would have in a bankruptcy proceeding. J.P. Morgan Chase agreed to honor all of Bear Stearns' contractual obligations, however, which meant that creditors and counterparties were fully compensated, creating moral hazard problems.

The main stumbling block for J.P. Morgan Chase was Bear Stearns' large portfolio of troubled assets. As part of the agreement, the Fed agreed to purchase up to $30 billion of Bear Stearns' assets through Maiden Lane I, a new Limited Liability Corporation (LLC) based in Delaware that it created and controlled. J.P. Morgan Chase would bear up to $1.15 billion in future first losses, based on assets valued at $29.97 billion at marked-to-market prices by Bear Stearns on March 14, 2008.[170] About half of these assets were collateralized mortgage obligations. The Fed has gradually sold off the assets, in order "to minimize disruption to financial markets and maximize recovery value."[171] This transaction exposed the Fed to significant credit risk on its balance sheet for the first time in decades. By 2012, Maiden Lane had received more from asset sales than the Fed had contributed to their purchases. Principal and interest were recouped, and some assets remained that could provide the Fed with additional future profits when sold. CBO estimated at the time of inception that the Maiden Lane transaction was not subsidized since the assets were bought at market prices.[172] In addition, during the JP Morgan Chase takeover, Bear Stearns had an average of $13.9 billion loans outstanding from the Primary Dealer Credit Facility from March 17 to June 23, 2008, and $1.5 billion loans outstanding from the Term Securities Lending Facility from March 28 to May 9, 2008.[173] These facilities were broadly based emergency Fed programs created during the crisis. These loans were repaid in full with interest.

Had Bear Stearns been a BHC, it might have been able to boost its liquidity with collateralized loans from the Fed. It also would have been subject to prudential regulation by the Fed that might have required it to pursue a more conservative business strategy. Since it was not a BHC, the Fed relied on emergency lending powers not used to lend to non-banks since the Great Depression. Since these powers limited the Fed to lending, the Fed was required to set up the LLC structure to make the asset purchases possible.

Although Bear Stearns' liquidity problems were driving it into bankruptcy had the government not interceded, it is unclear whether it was insolvent. Before that weekend, Bear Stearns was not insolvent by two common measurements: its stock price (representing the current market valuation of the firm's net worth) was still $30 per share, and its primary regulator, the Securities and Exchange Commission (SEC), issued a press release on March 11 that stated that Bear Stearns was adequately capitalized according to its net capital rule.[174] Even after the crisis, existing shares were valued positively in the J.P. Morgan Chase takeover, and no capital was provided to Bear Stearns as part of the Fed's assistance (since the assets bought by Maiden Lane were purchased at market value, according to the Fed). On the other hand, J.P. Morgan stated that the equity in Bear Stearns was exhausted and J.P. Morgan Chase took additional losses from costs associated with the Bear Stearns acquisition.[175]

Unlike the LTCM experience, the rescue of Bear Stearns arguably did not cause investors to conclude that Bear Stearns was an isolated "bad apple." Instead, speculation persisted over the next few months that other investment banks would suffer the same fate—speculation that came to a head with the wave of financial firm failures in September 2008.

Ban on Naked Short Selling in July 2008

As financial turmoil worsened in the summer of 2008, the stock value of many large financial firms fell quickly. The SEC responded on July 15, 2008, by announcing that investors would no longer be able to "naked short sell" the stocks of 19 large financial firms, an investment strategy that would pay off if the firms' stock price fell further.[176] The firms chosen were Fannie Mae, Freddie Mac, and the primary dealers (large financial firms that conduct open market operations with the Federal Reserve).[177] Some market participants perceived this announcement as an explicit list of the firms that the government considered too big to fail. If this announcement was intended to rescue troubled firms, either by making short selling more difficult or by making too big to fail status more explicit, it did not work in all cases—in September 2008, Lehman Brothers entered bankruptcy, while Fannie Mae and Freddie Mac entered government conservatorship. Nor did the list closely correspond to which firms would or would not receive government assistance subsequently—American International Group (AIG) received assistance although it was not one of the 19 firms listed, while Lehman Brothers did not receive although it was included on the list.

The July ban was superseded by an SEC rule issued on September 18, 2008, that temporarily banned all short-selling of the stocks of 700 financial firms and an October 1, 2008, rule that imposed a permanent ban on naked short-selling.

Fannie Mae and Freddie Mac

Not only were Fannie Mae and Freddie Mac very large, their TBTF status was also influenced by their unusual status as government sponsored enterprises (GSEs). Because of unusual features such as their congressional charter, line of credit with the Treasury, dominance of the home mortgage secondary market, and original status as government agencies, investors perceived them as more likely to be backed by the government than other firms, although their securities had no explicit government guarantee. This perception allowed them to consistently borrow at a lower cost than other financial firms, despite holding relatively little capital. Before conservatorship, Fannie Mae and Freddie Mac were the only firms regulated by their federal regulator, whose independence and powers were limited compared to other regulators.[178] These institutional features led critics to argue that the GSEs enjoyed the benefits of "regulatory capture." Their regulator found them to meet the statutory definition of well capitalized as recently as July 2008.[179]

Holding mainly mortgage-backed securities and mortgages in their portfolios, they were uniquely vulnerable to the decline in the housing market and MBS prices. In July 2008, investor concern about persistent losses and the potential for future losses led to a sharp decline in stock prices and cast doubt on their ability to roll over maturing debt. Treasury Secretary Paulson argued that the solution to this problem was for Congress to grant him what he referred to as a "bazooka"— the authority for Treasury to provide the GSEs with unlimited funding. He argued that the bazooka would calm investor fears, and as a result would not need to be used. Congress provided this authority in the Housing and Economic Recovery Act (P.L. 110-289).

By September 2008, the government decided to take the GSEs into conservatorship following further losses.[180] Conservatorship means that the government has assumed the normal powers of the officers, board of directors, and shareholders, but the GSEs would continue business operations. In addition, the government would purchase their MBS and inject as much capital as needed to keep the firms solvent. In return, the government received warrants to purchase 79.9% of the companies' common stock, which would dilute existing shareholders when exercised. Management was also replaced and dividends on preferred shares were eliminated, but creditors, including subordinated debt holders, and counterparties suffered no losses.

One rationale for placing the GSEs in conservatorship was that their dominant role in mortgage-backed securities markets could not have been replaced quickly by the private sector given the housing downturn. Without them, mortgage credit would have become less available, placing further downward pressure on the housing market. Another rationale was the potential for contagion to counterparties and creditors given the large amount of GSE debt and GSEguaranteed MBS outstanding.

To bridge the gap between the companies' assets and liabilities, the government provided $187.5 billion to the companies in exchange for preferred shares between 2008 and 2012. The government received $55 billion of dividends on those shares through 2012. Since then, the GSEs' assets have matched their liabilities and no further preferred share issuance has been needed. Under the existing agreement, the GSEs' profits (after dividend payments) would have accumulated in their coffers.[181] Treasury announced in August 2012 that, "(a)cting upon the commitment ... that the GSEs will be wound down and will not be allowed to retain profits, rebuild capital, and return to the market in their prior form," the preferred share agreements had been amended to replace the dividend and commitment fee with a "net income sweep" that would remit all profits to the Treasury.[182] Regardless of the amount remitted, the terms of the sweep do not allow for a reduction in the preferred shares outstanding. Thus, while Treasury has not recouped any principal, it earned a cumulative $202.8 billion in income through the first quarter of 2014—more than it outlayed.

In economic terms, the subsidy to the GSEs, which takes into account future losses and the opportunity cost inherent in the GSEs' ability to borrow at below market rates, was estimated by CBO to be $291 billion through 2009. Since this estimate was made in August 2009, the state of the housing market has improved considerably, which could reduce expected defaults and thus the size of the subsidy, were CBO to update its estimate. In addition, CBO assumes that the companies will continue to do business at below-market costs in the future that will lead to future subsidies from the government.[183]

Between December 2008 and March 2010, the Fed purchased $67 billion of debt issued by Freddie Mac and $67 billion issued by Fannie Mae as part of its "Large Scale Asset Purchases" (popularly known as quantitative easing). While the asset purchases were intended to provide support to mortgage markets and to stimulate overall economic conditions, another effect of these purchases was to reduce the GSEs' borrowing costs, all else equal. As these assets have matured, the Fed's holdings have declined over time. The Fed faces no default risk on its GSE holdings as long as the Treasury continues to stand behind the GSEs, and will not experience capital losses (or gains) as long as it continues to hold the securities to maturity. The Treasury and Fed have also purchased debt and MBS issued by the GSEs since 2008. The MBS purchases were made at market prices on the secondary market, so the purchases conferred no direct benefit to the GSEs, but had the effect of indirectly raising the price received by the GSEs for their MBS.

Lehman Brothers

Shortly after the failures of Fannie Mae and Freddie Mac, the investment bank Lehman Brothers experienced a liquidity crisis. Lehman Brothers was the 47th-largest firm by revenues in 2007 on *Fortune Magazine*'s Fortune 500 list.[184] Lehman Brothers was not a BHC regulated for safety and soundness, nor subject to the FDIC's resolution regime. Lehman Brothers was a unitary thrift holding company under OTS umbrella supervision; OTS was focused mainly on the health of the depository subsidiaries. It also complied with an SEC net capital rule.[185] Policy makers decided to allow Lehman Brothers to file for bankruptcy when it became clear that no other firm was willing to acquire the firm without government assistance. According to Bankruptcydata.com, Lehman Brothers was the largest firm by assets ever to file for bankruptcy.[186]

Lehman Brothers was larger than Bear Stearns and was involved in similar business lines. Bear Stearns had been saved with government assistance, and many market participants were surprised that a similar arrangement was not made for Lehman Brothers. Unlike Bear Stearns, Lehman Brothers had access to Fed lending facilities (created after the Bear Stearns crisis), but did not have enough collateral under the terms of the Fed program to borrow enough to meet its liquidity needs at the time of its failure. (This problem did not arise when the Fed rescued AIG the next day.) Policy makers argued that markets should not have expected government assistance because they had stressed since the Bear Stearns intervention that similar assistance could not be expected in the future and that failures were necessary to prevent moral hazard problems. Policy makers also argued that Lehman Brothers had plenty of time to defend themselves from the fate suffered by Bear Stearns by raising more capital and long-term liquidity. (Lehman Brothers did raise some in the summer of 2008.) Policy makers believed that they and counterparties were now well enough prepared for a counterparty failure that systemic risk could be contained.[187]

Some point to the complex, lengthy nature of Lehman Brothers' bankruptcy proceedings as evidence that Lehman Brothers was too big to fail, while others argue that bankruptcy proceedings have gone relatively smoothly and are successfully resolving the claims of creditors and counterparties in an orderly fashion.[188] A New York Fed study finds that creditors received an unusually low recovery rate from the Lehman bankruptcy.[189]

Where Lehman Brothers' failure proved more disruptive to financial markets was through its effects on money market mutual funds (MMF) and the commercial paper market. On September 16, 2008, a MMF called the Reserve Fund "broke the buck," meaning that the value of its shares had fallen below face value. This occurred because of losses it had taken on short-term debt issued by Lehman Brothers, which filed for bankruptcy on September 15, 2008. Money market investors had perceived "breaking the buck" to be highly unlikely, and its occurrence set off a run on money market funds, as investors simultaneously attempted to withdraw an estimated $250 billion of their investments—even from funds without exposure to Lehman Brothers.[190] MMFs are major investors in commercial paper, so this run greatly decreased the demand for new commercial paper.[191] Firms rely on the ability to issue new debt to roll over maturing debt to meet their liquidity needs. A blanket federal guarantee of MMFs and three Federal Reserve commercial paper programs were created to restore calm to these markets.[192]

Contagion from Lehman Brothers' failure also spread to its three remaining independent "bulge bracket" investment bank rivals, Merrill Lynch, Morgan Stanley, and Goldman Sachs. All three experienced liquidity strains following Lehman Brothers' failure, which all three survived, but only after fundamental changes to their business models. Merrill Lynch merged with Bank of America under financial strain, which would cause problems for Bank of America in the ensuing months. Goldman Sachs and Morgan Stanley changed their charters to become BHCs, under the umbrella supervision of the Federal Reserve. All three relied heavily on broadly based federal facilities to weather the storm. Borrowing from the Fed's Primary Dealer Credit Facility peaked at $48 billion for Morgan Stanley and $40 billion for Merrill Lynch on September 26, 2008, and at $17 billion for Goldman Sachs on October 10, 2008. All three firms also accessed the Fed's Term Securities Lending Facility throughout the fall and its Commercial Paper Funding Facility beginning in late October. Morgan Stanley and Goldman Sachs each received $10 billion in exchange for preferred shares through TARP's Capital Purchase Program on October 28, 2008, and $10 billion of CPP funds for Merrill Lynch were received by Bank of America after their merger.

Although the Fed was not willing to rescue Lehman Brothers, it provided Lehman Brothers with liquidity for a short time to ease the bankruptcy process.[193] Lehman Brothers borrowed an average of $23 billion each day from the Fed's Primary Dealer Credit Facility, a broadly based emergency facility, from September 15, the day it filed for bankruptcy, to September 17,

2008.[194] Lehman Brothers also borrowed from the Fed's Term Securities Lending Facility frequently from March 2008 to September 12, 2008.

AIG

At the same time as the failure of Lehman Brothers, American International Group (AIG) ran into liquidity problems as a result of collateral calls on its credit default swaps and securities lending program.[195]

AIG is a large financial firm operating domestically and abroad; at the time of the crisis, its insurance operations were the fifth largest in the world. While AIG is often thought of as an insurance company, it was a complex financial institution with many different types of subsidiaries, such as AIG Financial Products, which Fed Chairman Bernanke reportedly likened to a hedge fund.[196] Its overall legal structure was a unitary thrift regulated by the Office of Thrift Supervision (OTS), although its thrift operations were relatively small. AIG's insurance subsidiaries were regulated at the state level. Losses were centered in the Financial Products subsidiary and its securities lending program; as its umbrella regulator, OTS was focused mainly on the health of the depository subsidiaries. OTS has testified that it did not fully foresee the potential losses that transactions undertaken by AIG Financial Products posed to the holding company.[197]

Unlike Lehman Brothers, policy makers decided that the systemic risk implications of an AIG failure were too great. AIG was listed as the 10th-largest firm by revenues in 2007 on *Fortune Magazine*'s Fortune 500 list.[198] On September 16, 2008, the Fed announced that it was taking action to support AIG. Using emergency authority, this support took the form of a secured two-year line of credit with a value of up to $85 billion and a high interest rate (set at 8.5 percentage points above the London Interbank Offered Rate). Although the Fed denied assistance to Lehman Brothers on the grounds that it lacked acceptable collateral, the loan to AIG was collateralized by the general assets of AIG.[199] In addition, the government received warrants to purchase up to 79.9% of the equity in AIG.

Once the determination to assist AIG had been made, assistance arguably became open-ended, and more government assistance was provided on several subsequent occasions. On October 8, 2008, the Fed announced that it would lend AIG up to an additional $37.8 billion against securities held by its insurance subsidiaries. These securities had been previously lent out and were not available as collateral at the time of the original intervention, increasing AIG's cash flow problems. In October 2008, AIG also announced that it had applied to the Fed's general Commercial Paper Facility and was approved to borrow up to $20.9 billion at the facility's standard terms.

The financial support for AIG was restructured in early November 2008. The restructured financial support included up to a $60 billion loan from the Fed, with the term lengthened to five years and the interest rate reduced by 5.5 percentage points; $40 billion in preferred share purchases through the TARP through a new program created for AIG called the "Systemically Significant Failing Institutions Program"; up to $52.5 billion total in asset purchases by the Fed through two Limited Liability Corporations (LLCs) known as Maiden Lane II and Maiden Lane III. AIG contributed an additional $6 billion for the LLCs and will bear the first $6 billion in any losses on the asset values. By 2012, the Maiden Lanes had received more from asset sales than the Fed had contributed to their purchases. Principal and interest were recouped, and further gains from these LLCs were shared between the Fed and AIG.

The 79.9% common equity position of the government in AIG remained essentially unchanged after the restructuring of the intervention, although assistance was increased. Additional restructurings were announced in March 2010 and September 2010. In the latter restructuring, the Federal Reserve loan was repaid in full and the preferred shares were converted into common equity. This increases the risk and potential reward for the government from its AIG holdings since the common equity can rise or fall in value based on market conditions and the future financial performance of AIG. Warrants initially valued at $1.2 billion were also issued to AIG's private shareholders at this time, transferring value from the government to shareholders. The government sold its common equity stake between May 2011 and December 2012.

With each restructuring, costs were reduced for AIG and risks were shifted away from AIG to the government. Policy makers initially provided loans with very high interest rates out of moral hazard concerns, but found that punitive conditions decreased the ongoing viability of the company (and, hence, the probability that the assistance would be repaid). Therefore, when assistance was revised, conditions typically became less punitive. Since the government held 92.6% of the common stock in AIG at the peak, however, a case can be made that the benefits of any restructuring that improves AIG's future profitability mostly accrues to the government.

On a cash-flow basis, the Fed and Treasury combined ultimately received $23 billion more than they outlayed to AIG. Whether this resulted in an economic profit for the federal government or a subsidy to AIG depends on the opportunity cost of those funds, based on the risks that the government undertook and the time value of money. CBO has made such a calculation, and estimates that the TARP portion of the assistance to AIG will have a net cost of $15 billion over the lifetime of the assistance.[200] At the time of the Fed's intervention, CBO estimated a $2 billion subsidy for the Fed portion of the assistance; since the Fed's intervention turned out to be cash-flow positive and CBO has revised downward its estimates of TARP subsidies over time, that amount could be re-estimated downward if CBO were to update it.

Washington Mutual and Wachovia

Two large banks, Washington Mutual and Wachovia, were successfully resolved by the FDIC through mergers during the 2008 crisis, at no cost to the taxpayers.

Washington Mutual was a thrift holding company. Its depository subsidiary experienced depositor runs in 2008 following losses. It was the 81st-largest firm by revenues in 2007 on *Fortune Magazine*'s Fortune 500 list and the largest thrift holding company.[201] Depositors withdrew $9.4 billion between July 12 and July 30, and $15 billion between September 11 and 26—the closest the 2008 crisis saw to a traditional bank run.[202] On September 25, the thrift was taken into receivership by the FDIC. It was resolved through a purchase and assumption agreement with J.P. Morgan Chase. As part of the agreement, J.P. Morgan Chase paid $1.9 billion to assume the claims of uninsured depositors, counterparties with qualified financial contracts, and secured creditors; it did not assume the claims of unsecured creditors or equity holders.[203] The remainder of the company filed for bankruptcy on September 26. Thus, the receivership required no federal funds, and the moral hazard problem was mitigated since unsecured creditors and equity holders suffered losses. J.P. Morgan Chase's willingness to pay to assume other liabilities implies that it believed the remaining assets were sufficient to honor those liabilities.

Washington Mutual received a $1 billion, 28-day loan from the Federal Reserve's Term Auction Facility on September 11, 2008. The bank was closed by the FDIC on September 25, 2008, and the loan was repaid after its merger. Since the loan was fully collateralized and the Fed receives priority ahead of other creditors, it appears to have posed little risk to the taxpayers in the face of receivership. Nonetheless, the loan appears to have been a departure from Fed policy since the Fed's broadly based lending programs were intended to provide liquidity to solvent firms.

Washington Mutual could be seen as an example of a TBTF bank that experienced an orderly resolution through the FDIC's resolution regime at no cost to the taxpayers. Or it could be seen as too small to be relevant to the TBTF debate.

Wachovia (the 46th-largest firm on *Fortune Magazine*'s Fortune 500 list in 2007) faced runs soon after Washington Mutual failed. According to Federal Reserve testimony,

> The day after the failure of WaMu, Wachovia Bank depositors accelerated the withdrawal of significant amounts from their accounts. In addition, wholesale funds providers withdrew liquidity support from Wachovia. It appeared likely that Wachovia would soon become unable to fund its operations.[204]

According to the Fed, problems at Wachovia were unforeseen, making the bank both a victim and a potential transmitter of contagion:

> At the time, Wachovia was considered "well capitalized" by regulatory standards and until very recently had not generally been thought to be in danger of failure, so there were fears that the failure of Wachovia would lead investors to doubt the financial strength of other organizations in similar situations, making it harder for those institutions to raise capital and other funding.[205]

On September 27 and 28, Wells Fargo and Citigroup placed competing bids to acquire Wachovia. Initially, those bids were contingent on federal assistance. FDIC assistance under the systemic risk exception to least cost resolution had been approved.[206] Later, Wells Fargo revised its offer, acquiring Wachovia without federal assistance and averting a receivership.

Neither the Washington Mutual nor the Wachovia acquisitions were found to breach the RiegleNeal 10% nationwide deposit cap. JP Morgan Chase's acquisition of Washington Mutual's deposits and other assets occurred through an FDIC purchase and assumption arrangement. The 10% deposit cap does not apply to an FDIC purchase and assumption. In its approval of Wells Fargo's acquisition of Wachovia, the Fed noted that using the most current data, the merged entity would be above the 10% deposit limit. The Fed then argued that since that data were released with a lag, projections of *current* deposit data indicated that the merger would probably fall below the 10% cap.[207]

Although the Fed's Term Auction Facility was intended for healthy firms, Wachovia received nine Term Auction Facility loans between September 11, 2008, and February 26, 2009, including $5 billion on September 25, 2008, one day before the run on Wachovia began. Its merger with Wells Fargo was announced on October 3, 2008.

TARP, Citigroup, Bank of America, and the Stress Tests

The first and largest program initiated under the Troubled Asset Relief Program (TARP) was the Capital Purchase Program (CPP).[208] The purpose of the CPP was to provide banks and BHCs with preferred shares to increase their capital buffers against future losses at a time when it was difficult for banks to access private capital. The CPP was intended for healthy banks of all sizes and unsuitable candidates were rejected. Therefore, it does not closely match the definition of bailout used in this report, which implies assistance to unhealthy firms, or TBTF assistance. Nevertheless, CPP funds went to banks that later failed (14 mostly small banks, as of December 2011)[209] and the first recipients were the nine largest BHCs, all of whom had fully repaid CPP shares by 2010. If limited to healthy banks and purchased at market rates, preferred shares impose limited risk on taxpayers. Despite the handful of losses on CPP investments in small banks, CBO has estimated that the government will ultimately earn an overall economic profit (i.e., earn an above market rate of return) from the CPP from dividends and warrants. In October 2012, CBO estimated that profit to be $18 billion.[210]

After the initial disbursement of CPP funds, Citigroup and Bank of America received additional TARP capital injections and asset guarantees for their balance sheet holdings through a special TARP program with no other recipients. The additional capital paid a higher dividend rate than the CPP shares. Other TARP programs included programs to assist AIG (discussed above) and the automakers. As will be discussed, the program for automakers was used to provide special assistance to two financial firms, Chrysler Financial and GMAC (later renamed Ally Financial).

Following the additional TARP capital injections, Citigroup remained well capitalized according to regulatory standards.[211] It appears that without TARP funds Citigroup would have fallen to slightly below the Fed's minimum Tier 1 Leverage requirements of 4% at the end of 2008, assuming they had not raised private capital in the absence of TARP funds.[212] Regulations require BHCs to submit a plan to the Fed in a timely manner if they fall below minimum capital requirements.[213] In February 2009, Citigroup and the federal government reached an agreement to convert up to $27.5 billion of Citigroup's TARP preferred shares into common equity. This agreement had the result of boosting Citigroup's common equity ratios and ending dividend payments to the government.[214] It also exposed the government to greater risk and potentially greater return on its investments, since common equity can rise and fall in value, unlike the TARP preferred shares. Citigroup was the largest financial firm in the country and eighth-largest firm overall on *Fortune Magazine*'s 2007 Fortune 500 list.[215]

Bank of America's financial problems centered mainly on its acquisitions of Countrywide and another very large financial firm, the investment bank Merrill Lynch. At the time of the Lehman Brothers crisis, Merrill Lynch also came under financial pressure as a result of its similar business model, forcing it to seek a merger partner. Merrill Lynch (the 22nd-largest firm on *Fortune Magazine*'s Fortune 500 list in 2007) was larger than either of those firms. In September 2008, Bank of America and Merrill Lynch reached an agreement in principle to merge. As financial conditions deteriorated further, Bank of America considered pulling out of the merger. To prevent this, according to the Treasury Secretary at the time, the government agreed to purchase another $20 billion of preferred shares through TARP and enter into a federal asset guarantee agreement.[216] The merger was finalized in January 2009, and Bank of America received the additional TARP shares shortly thereafter; the asset guarantee was never finalized. In its March 2009 call report, Bank of America remained well capitalized according to regulatory standards.[217] It appears that even without TARP funds Bank of America would have remained above the Fed's minimum Tier 1 leverage requirements of 4% in that quarter.[218]

In May 2009, the Federal Reserve released the results of the Supervisory Capital Assessment Program, its "stress tests" for the 19 largest BHCs.[219] The stress tests were meant to determine whether these banks would remain well capitalized in the event of a downside economic scenario. The tests required banks to be able to maintain Tier 1 Risk-Based Capital of 6% and Tier 1 Common Capital of 4% in this scenario. Of the participants, 10 of 19 were found to be well capitalized against future losses; of those 10, the 9 participating in TARP bought back their preferred shares and exited the program shortly thereafter. Of the other nine that required additional capital to withstand hypothetical losses under the adverse scenario, seven (including Bank of America, which was required to raised $33.9 billion) were able to raise the needed capital without government funds; GMAC required TARP funds (through the Automotive Industry Financing Program) to raise the needed capital; and Citigroup, which was required to raise $5.5 billion, met the threshold for Tier 1 Common Capital in part by converting more of its existing CPP preferred shares into common shares. After the preferred shares were converted to common equity, the government owned about one-third of the company.[220]

In December 2009, Citigroup bought back $20 billion of TARP preferred securities outstanding, replacing those shares with private capital, and terminated the government's asset guarantee for a fee. In March 2010, the Treasury announced plans to dispose of its common shares in Citigroup by the end of the year. The government ultimately sold these shares for $31.9 billion, or $6.9 billion more than the initial assistance extended. Treasury reports that for the three programs assisting Citigroup combined, it had a positive cash flow of $13.4 billion.[221]

In December 2009, Bank of America repurchased all of its TARP preferred shares, replacing those shares with private capital, and paid a fee to cancel the asset guarantee that was negotiated but never entered into.

The experience with Bank of America and Citigroup is quite different from the experience with AIG and the GSEs. While TARP funds kept Bank of America's and Citigroup's capital levels above the minimally required level, neither firm is believed to have been close to insolvency — although it is unknown what would have happened to Merrill Lynch had Bank of America not acquired it. Bank of America repaid TARP funds in full in December 2009, and the government fully divested from Citigroup in 2010. CBO has estimated that the government earned an economic profit, calculated using a risk-adjusted discount rate, of $8 billion from its special assistance to the two companies.[222]

GMAC

While Congress authorized TARP to "purchase, and to make and fund commitments to purchase, troubled assets from any financial institution, on such terms and conditions as are determined by the Secretary, and in accordance with this Act and the policies and procedures developed and published by the Secretary," TARP funding was also used to facilitate the bankruptcy process for GM and Chrysler.[223] Economists have generally focused on financial firms as being TBTF because of the interconnectedness inherent in financial intermediation; determining whether automakers can be TBTF is beyond the scope of this report.

In conjunction with the automakers, two financial firms related to the automakers, GMAC and Chrysler Financial, also received TARP assistance. Chrysler Financial was a relatively small financial firm, and it repaid its $1.5 billion TARP loan in full with interest by July 2009. GMAC received several rounds of TARP funding in order to return its capital levels to acceptable levels. After converting to a BHC during the crisis, GMAC was the 10th-largest BHC, with $180 billion in assets, in the first quarter of 2009. It dominated dealer floorplan financing for GM and Chrysler, and reportedly had three times the market share of its five largest competitors in auto financing.[224]

TARP first purchased $5 billion of GMAC preferred shares in December 2008 and lent $884 million to GM, which was later transferred to GMAC, as part of the initial assistance provided to the automakers. As discussed above, GMAC was one of the nine BHCs that were required to raise additional capital under the May 2009 stress tests. It was the only one of those nine that raised the capital through additional TARP disbursements, rather than through private markets. The government purchased an additional $7.5 billion of preferred shares and converted the $884 million loan into 35.4% of GMAC's common equity in May 2009. The government then purchased $2.54 billion of trust preferred securities and an additional $1.25 billion of preferred shares in December 2009. At the same time, it converted $3 billion in preferred shares for 20.9% of GMAC's common equity. In December 2010, it converted an additional $5.5 billion of preferred shares into 17.5% of GMAC's common equity; $5.9 billion of preferred shares remain outstanding, and the government has sold the trust preferred securities to private investors at face value. This made recoupment of funds for the government dependent on the future value of GMAC (renamed Ally Financial).225 To date, the government has sold its preferred shares back to GMAC and some of its common stock to private investors. Although the government still holds shares, the proceeds from share sales plus income received less writeoffs to date has slightly exceeded its total initial outlays. CBO does not estimate a separate subsidy cost for the government's assistance to GMAC, but estimates "a small net cost" for assistance to GMAC and Chrysler Financial combined.[226]

End Notes

[1] For more information, see CRS Report R41073, *Government Interventions in Response to Financial Turmoil*, by Baird Webel and Marc Labonte.

[2] For an overview, see CRS Report R41350, *The Dodd-Frank Wall Street Reform and Consumer Protection Act: Background and Summary*, coordinated by Baird Webel. For more information on systemic risk provisions, see CRS Report R41384 *The Dodd-Frank Wall Street Reform and Consumer Protection Act: Systemic Risk and the Federal Reserve*, by Marc Labonte.

[3] For more information on the FSOC, see CRS Report R42083, *Financial Stability Oversight Council: A Framework to Mitigate Systemic Risk*, by Edward V. Murphy.

[4] Information on designated firms can be accessed at http://www.treasury.gov/initiatives/fsoc/designations/Pages/ default.aspx.

[5] The complaint can be accessed at http://online.wsj.com/public/resources/ documents/011315metlife.pdf. For more information, see CRS Report WSLG1164, *MetLife's SIFI Designation Goes to Court*, by M. Maureen Murphy.

[6] GE, Conference Call (Transcript), April 10, 2015, http://www.ge.com/sites/default/files/ ge_webcast_transcript_04102015_0.pdf.

[7] Financial Stability Board (FSB), "2014 Update of Global Systemically Important Banks," November 6, 2014, http://www.financialstabilityboard.org/wp-content/uploads/ r_141106b. pdf; FSB, "2014 Update of List of Global Systemically Important Insurers," November 6, 2014, http://www.financialstabilityboard.org/wp-content/uploads/ r_141106a.pdf. The FSB is an international forum of which the United States is a member.

[8] See, for example, Government Accountability Office, *Large Bank Holding Companies – Expectations of Government Support*, GAO-14-621, July 2014.

[9] Data from National Information Center, http://www.ffiec.gov/nicpubweb/nicweb/ Top50Form.aspx. This list includes any type of institution that includes a depository subsidiary. These data exaggerate changes in the relative importance of large banks since they do not take into account inflation or growth in the economy.

[10] Federal Reserve Bank of Chicago, *Top Banks and Holding Companies*, period ending June 30, 2014, available at http://www.chicagofed.org/webpages/ banking/financial_institution_ reports/top_banks_bhcs.cfm. In addition, the top five savings and loan holding companies hold 66% of total assets and the top five state-member banks hold 47% of total assets; banks in those categories are considerably smaller in absolute terms than bank holding companies (BHCs), however.

[11] Andrew Haldane and Robert May, "Systemic Risk in Banking Ecosystems," *Nature*, vol. 469, January 2011, p. 351.

[12] Organization of Economic Cooperation and Development, *Bank Competition and Financial Stability*, 2011, Figure 1.1.

[13] Many of these large institutions that focus on non-banking activities are chartered as BHCs or savings and loan holding companies.

[14] For more information, see CRS Report R43345, *Shadow Banking: Background and Policy Issues*, by Edward V. Murphy and Tobias Adrian, Adam Ashcraft, and Zoltan Pozsar, "Shadow Banking," Federal Reserve Bank of New York, working paper, December 31, 2009.

[15] Tobias Adrian, Christopher Burke, and James McAndrews, *The Federal Reserve's Primary Dealer Credit Facility*, Federal Reserve Bank of New York, Current Issues in Economics and Finance, vol. 15, no. 4, New York, NY, August 2009.

[16] According to one estimate, mergers and acquisitions during the crisis increased the assets of the four largest banks from 30% to 44% of total bank assets. Richard Fisher, "Two Areas of Present Concern," speech before the Senior Delegates' Roundtable of the Fixed Income Forum, Federal Reserve Bank of Dallas, July 23, 2009.

[17] Data can be accessed at http://money.cnn.com/magazines/fortune/fortune500/. The lack of financial firms in the top 10 by revenue does not appear to be driven by the effects of the financial crisis. For example, there were two predominantly financial firms in the top 10 by revenue in 2006.

[18] One study of the ten most concentrated industries did not include any financial firms. See Andrea Alegria *et al*, "Highly Concentrated: Companies that Dominate Their Industries," *IBISWorld*, February 2012, http://www.ibisworld.com/Common/MediaCenter/Highly%20 Concentrated%20Industries.pdf.

[19] An alternative perspective is that the simultaneous failure or emergency experienced by many firms during the crisis was primarily caused by a lack of diversified risk that led to many firms experiencing losses on similar investments (in this case, mortgage-related investments), as opposed to losses being caused by counterparty exposure. This perspective does not necessarily require a TBTF problem to explain the crisis. For example, see Daniel Tarullo, "Regulating Systemic Risk," speech at 2011 Credit Markets Symposium, Charlotte, North Carolina, March 31, 2011, http://www.federalreserve.gov/newsevents/speech/tarullo20110331a.htm.

[20] Hereafter, for convenience, this report will use the terms "too big to fail" and "too interconnected to fail" interchangeably.

[21] International Monetary Fund, *United States—Selected Issues*, July 13, 2009, p. 24.

[22] See, for example, Financial Crisis Inquiry Commission, *Final Report*, chap. 18, http://fcic-static.law.stanford.edu/ cdn_media/fcic-reports/fcic_final_report_full.pdf. For an alternative perspective on the importance of Lehman Brothers, see "Dissenting Views" in the same report.

[23] For more information on the events of 2008, see the Appendix.

[24] In the case of Fannie Mae and Freddie Mac, this was arguably the policy goal—Fannie Mae's and Freddie Mac's low-borrowing costs were seen by some as desirable insofar as it led to lower borrowing costs for homeowners. A key feature of the housing bubble was overinvestment in housing, spurred by the over-availability of mortgage credit.

[25] Evidence that larger banks are consistently riskier than smaller banks is mixed. For example, one measure of riskiness is leverage (the proportion of liabilities to equity held by a bank). One study found that large U.S. commercial banks were less leveraged than small banks on average during the past decade, but the median large bank was modestly more leveraged than the median small bank. Large banks also had more off-balance-sheet activities, which some believe made banks appear to be less risky than they turned out to be. The study also found that investment banks were much more leveraged than commercial banks, and large investment banks were more leveraged than small ones. Source: Sebnem Kalemli-Ozcan, Bent Sorensen, Sevcan Yesiltas, "Leverage Across Firms, Banks, and Countries," National Bureau of Economic Research, working paper no. 17354, August 2011. Anecdotal evidence points to a number of large banks whose risky behavior resulted in failure or rescue during the crisis, but most failing banks over the past few years were small banks.

[26] Economists refer to this as a "principal-agent" problem.

[27] Studies using empirical evidence to estimate the TBTF funding advantage are reviewed in Financial Crisis Inquiry Commission, "Governmental Rescues of 'Too Big To Fail' Financial Institutions," Preliminary Staff Report, August 2010, chap. 3, http://fcic-static.law.stanford.edu/cdn_media/fcic-reports/2010-0831-Governmental-Rescues.pdf; Randall Kroszner, "A Review of Bank Funding Cost Differentials," University of Chicago, working paper, November 2013, https://www.stern.nyu.edu/sites/default/files/assets/documents/con_044532.pdf; Thomas Hoenig, Testimony before the Committee on Financial Services, U.S. House of Representatives, June 26, 2013, Attachment 3, http://financialservices.house.gov/uploadedfiles/hhrg-113-ba00-wstate-thoenig-20130626.pdf.

[28] See Goldman Sachs, "Measuring the TBTF Effect on Bond Pricing," *Global Markets Institute*, May 2013.

[29] Government Accountability Office, *Large Bank Holding Companies – Expectations of Government Support*, GAO-14-621, July 2014, pp. 40-55.

[30] Government Accountability Office, *Large Bank Holding Companies – Expectations of Government Support*, GAO-14-621, July 2014, p. 24 and Financial Stability Oversight Council, *Annual Report*, 2014, p. 117.

[31] Financial Crisis Inquiry Commission, "Governmental Rescues of 'Too Big To Fail' Financial Institutions," Preliminary Staff Report, August 2010, chap. 3, http://fcic-static.law.stanford.edu/cdn_media/fcic-reports/2010-0831- Governmental-Rescues.pdf.

[32] An alternative perspective is that there was no explicit TBTF policy because changes in market structure over time— namely, the emergence of large, complex banks and non-bank financial firms—did not trigger legislative changes to create a TBTF policy.

[33] Thrifts, credit unions, and banks that did not have holding company structures were not subject to prudential oversight by the Fed. In this sense, some large banks were regulated differently than some small banks before the crisis, although not all BHCs were large and not all thrifts were small.

[34] Since there was no explicit TBTF policy, it is speculative as to whether the Fed considered all of the banks it identified as large complex banking institutions to be TBTF. Prior to the crisis, there was not authority to set higher quantitative prudential standards for TBTF banks, although regulators do enjoy discretion in their supervision. See Federal Reserve, *Framework for Risk-Focused Supervision of Large Complex Institutions*, Handbook, August 1997, http://www.federalreserve.gov/boarddocs/srletters/1997/sr9724a1.pdf.

[35] For more information, see Mark Greenlee, "Historical Review of 'Umbrella Regulation' by the Board of Governors of the Federal Reserve System," Federal Reserve Bank of Cleveland, working paper 08-07, October 2008.

[36] For more information, see "Selected Historical Experiences With "Too Big To Fail"

[37] For more information on the GSEs, see CRS Report RL34657, *Financial Institution Insolvency: Federal Authority over Fannie Mae, Freddie Mac, and Depository Institutions*.

[38] As discussed above, due to the nature of financial intermediation, financial firms can never hold enough liquidity to survive a run. Nevertheless, critics have argued that the Fed's response to turmoil enabled firms to take on excessive liquidity risk. This policy is sometimes referred to as the "Greenspan put," referring to the fact that the Fed's willingness to provide liquidity in times of trouble provided firms with a hedge against liquidity risk.

[39] 12 USC 1823(c). In total, GAO reports that the FDIC's systemic risk exception was invoked five times during the crisis. See Government Accountability Office, *Federal Deposit Insurance Act:Regulators' Use of Systemic Risk Exception*, GAO-10-100, April 2010.

[40] Information on government assistance provided during the crisis can be found in CRS Report R41073, *Government Interventions in Response to Financial Turmoil*, by Baird Webel and Marc Labonte.

[41] A GAO evaluation found that while the largest banks received a majority of the assistance from the Fed's broadly based emergency programs in dollar terms, they had the lowest ratio of assistance to total assets, whereas the smallest banks had the highest ratio. By contrast, the largest banks had the highest ratio of guaranteed debt to assets in the FDIC's TGLP and the highest ratio of capital to assets in TARP while participating. Government Accountability Office, *Government Support for Bank Holding Companies*, GAO-14-18, November 2013, Table 4, 5, and 6.

[42] See, for example, Financial Crisis Inquiry Commission, *Final Report*, chap. 18, http://fcic-static.law.stanford.edu/ cdn_media/fcic-reports/fcic_final_report_full.pdf; Congressional Oversight Panel, *An Overall Assessment of TARP and Financial Stability*, 112th Cong., 1st sess., March 4, 2011, S.Hrg.112-3. For an overview of government assistance during the

crisis, see CRS Report R43413, *Costs of Government Interventions in Response to the Financial Crisis: A Retrospective*, by Baird Webel and Marc Labonte.

[43] An alternative perspective is that government intervention worsened the crisis by creating policy uncertainty. See, for example, John Taylor, "The Financial Crisis and the Policy Responses: An Empirical Analysis of What Went Wrong," November 2008, working paper, http://www.stanford.edu/~johntayl/FCPR.pdf.

[44] As will be discussed in the section below entitled "Resolving a Large, Interconnected Failing Firm," the failure could be resolved by the bankruptcy process or a special receivership regime, similar to how banks are resolved. If the latter is used, then issues arise as to what government support becomes available to creditors through the receiver

[45] Economists refer to this as a "time inconsistency" problem. See Gary Stern and Ron Feldman, *Too Big to Fail*, Brookings Institute Press, Washington, D.C., 2004, chap. 2.

[46] Congressional Oversight Panel, *March Oversight Report*, March 16, 2011, p. 153, http://frwebgate.access.gpo.gov/ cgi-bin/getdoc.cgi?dbname=112_senate_hearings&docid=f:64832.pdf.

[47] See, for example, John Taylor, "The Financial Crisis and the Policy Responses: An Empirical Analysis of What Went Wrong," November 2008, working paper, http://www.stanford.edu/~johntayl/FCPR.pdf.

[48] For more information, see the Appendix.

[49] For example, CBO expected TARP alone to have a subsidy cost of $190 billion in January 2009. See Congressional Budget Office, *The Budget and Economic Outlook*, January 2009, p. 25.

[50] CRS Report R43413, *Costs of Government Interventions in Response to the Financial Crisis: A Retrospective*, by Baird Webel and Marc Labonte.

[51] Congressional Budget Office, *Report on the Troubled Asset Relief Program*, March 2015. There is no recent estimate of the economic costs for programs outside of TARP. Economic gains on assistance to AIG outside of TARP partly or wholly offset economic costs to AIG through TARP.

[52] An alternative perspective is that government intervention worsened the crisis by creating policy uncertainty. See, for example, John Taylor, "The Financial Crisis and the Policy Responses: An Empirical Analysis of What Went Wrong," November 2008, working paper, http://www.stanford.edu/~johntayl/FCPR.pdf.

[53] The Fed issued a proposed rule "Extensions of Credit by Federal Reserve Banks," January 6, 2014, available at http://www.federalreserve.gov/newsevents/press/bcreg/20131223a.htm.

[54] One variation on this approach would be to cap borrowing, so that a firm would face no size limit when financing its activities through capital, but in effect could not grow past a specified threshold through the use of leverage.

[55] Federal Deposit Insurance Corporation, "Continental Illinois and 'Too Big to Fail'," *History of the Eighties*, Ch. 7, http://www.fdic.gov/bank/historical/history/235_258.pdf. For more information, see the section below on Continental Illinois in the Appendix.

[56] See, for example, Anat R. Admati *et* al, "Fallacies, Irrelevant Facts, and Myths in the Discussion of Capital Regulation: Why Bank Equity is Not Expensive," working paper, March 23, 2011, https://gsbapps.stanford.edu/ researchpapers/library/RP2065R1&86.pdf.

[57] The evidence on the existence of economies of scale is reviewed in Inci Otker-Robe et al, "The Too-Important-to Fail Conundrum," International Monetary Fund, *Staff Discussion Note SGN/11/12*, May 2011, available at http://www.imf.org/external/pubs/ft/sdn/2011/sdn1112.pdf. See also David Wheelock and Paul Wilson, "Do Large Banks Have Lower Costs? New Estimates of Returns to Scale for U.S. Banks," Federal Reserve Bank of

St. Louis, Working Paper 2009-054E, May 2011, http://research.stlouisfed.org/wp/2009/2009-054.pdf.

[58] According to Hamilton Place Strategies, the largest syndicated loan in 2012 involved underwriting by the four largest U.S. banks and two foreign banks. See Hamilton Place Strategies, "Banking on Our Future," *HPSinsight*, February 2013.

[59] These benefits are also discussed in Hamilton Place Strategies, "Banking on Our Future," *HPSinsight*, February 2013.

[60] Financial Stability Oversight Council, *Study and Recommendations Regarding Concentration Limits on Large Financial Companies*, January 2011, http://www.treasury.gov/initiatives/Documents/Study%20on%20Concentration%20Limits%20on%20Large%20Firms%2001-17-11.pdf.

[61] See Thorsten Beck, "Bank Competition and Financial Stability, Friends or Foes?," in *Competition in the Financial Sector*, Bank Indonesia and Banco de Mexico, 2008; Antonio Ruiz-Porras, "Banking competition and financial fragility: Evidence from panel-data, *Estudios Economicos*, vol. 23, no. 1, 2008.

[62] See Renee Haltom, "Why Was Canada Exempt From the Financial Crisis?, *Economic* Focus, Fourth Quarter, 2013, p. 22.

[63] See Jeremy Stein, "Regulating Large Financial Institutions," speech at the International Monetary Fund, April 17, 2013.

[64] A final rule implementing the limit was released in November 2014. The rule, "Concentration Limits on Large Financial Companies," can be accessed at http://www.federalreserve.gov/newsevents/press/bcreg/20141105a.htm.

[65] Financial Stability Oversight Council, *Study and Recommendations Regarding Concentration Limits on Large Financial Companies*, January 2011, p. 8, http://www.treasury.gov/initiatives/Documents/Study%20on%20Concentration%20Limits%20on%20Large%20Firms%2001-17-11.pdf.

[66] For more information, see the Appendix.

[67] Tobias Adrian and Adam Ashcraft, "Shadow Banking: A Review of the Literature," Federal Reserve Bank of New York, Staff Report no. 580, October 2012.

[68] The Financial Stability Oversight Council has grappled with coming up with developing metrics for these concepts in its rulemaking (12 CFR Part 1310, RIN 4030-AA00). Different perspectives on defining the concepts can be found in the public comments to the rulemaking. See also International Monetary Fund, Bank for International Settlements, Financial Stability Board, *Guidance to Assess the Systemic Importance of Financial Institutions, Markets and Instruments*, report, October 2009, available at http://www.imf.org/external/np/g20/pdf/100109.pdf.

[69] Reinstating the Glass-Steagall Act in its entirety would involve many other policy areas as well that have changed significantly over time. Proponents of reinstating Glass-Steagall are usually understood to be focused on four key provisions. For more information, see CRS Report R41181, *Permissible Securities Activities of Commercial Banks Under the Glass-Steagall Act (GSA) and the Gramm-Leach-Bliley Act (GLBA)*, by David H. Carpenter and M. Maureen Murphy.

[70] Under current law, there are still limits on the types of business activities that banking subsidiaries can undertake, but non-banking subsidiaries within the same holding company may operate in different lines of financial business.

[71] Financial Stability Oversight Council, *Study and Recommendations on Prohibitions on Proprietary Trading*, January 2011, http://www.treasury.gov/initiatives/Documents/Volcker%20sec%20%20619%20study%20final%201%2018%2011%20rg.pdf.

[72] Thomas Hoenig and Charles Morris, "Restructuring the Banking System to Improve Safety and Soundness," Federal Reserve Bank of Kansas City, working paper, December 2012.

[73] Independent Commission on Banking, *Interim Report*, United Kingdom, April 2011.

[74] High-level Expert Group on Reforming the Structure of the EU banking Sector Chaired by Erkki Liikanen, *Final Report*, European Union, October 2, 2012.

[75] In the United States, some have argued that each subsidiary within a holding company should be made legally and operationally separate. See, for example, Sheila Bair, *Bull by the Horns*, Simon and Schuster, (New York, NY: 2012), p. 329; Brad Miller, "Use Stand-Alone Subsidiaries to Break Up Megabanks," *Wall Street Journal*, October 21, 2012.

[76] The term swaps refers to over-the-counter derivatives. It is statutorily defined in 7 U.S.C. 1a(47).

[77] Cady North, "Volcker Rule Risk Concentrated in 25 Banks," Bloomberg Government, October 14, 2011, p. 5.

[78] See American Bankers Association, *Letter to Alastair Fitzpayne: Information on the FSOC Notice 2010-0002*, November 3, 2010, http://www.aba.com/aba/documents/news/VolckerTrust11410.pdf; SIFMA, *Volcker Rule*, http://www.sifma.org/issues/regulatory-reform/volcker-rule/position/.

[79] For more information, see CRS Report R41298, *The "Volcker Rule": Proposals to Limit "Speculative" Proprietary Trading by Banks*, by David H. Carpenter and M. Maureen Murphy.

[80] The final rule, "Prohibitions and Restrictions on Proprietary Trading and Certain Interests in, and Relationships With, Hedge Funds and Private Equity Funds; Final Rule," is available at http://federalreserve.gov/newsevents/press/ bcreg/20131210a.htm.

[81] For more information, see CRS Report R41398, *The Dodd-Frank Wall Street Reform and Consumer Protection Act: Title VII, Derivatives*, by Rena S. Miller and Kathleen Ann Ruane.

[82] "Prohibition Against Federal Assistance to Swaps Entities," June 10, 2013, available at http://federalreserve.gov/ newsevents/press/bcreg/20130605a.htm.

[83] For more information, see CRS Report WSLG1135, *Will an Amendment to the Swaps "Pushout" Rule Push the "Cromnibus" to Defeat?*, by David H. Carpenter.

[84] The potential for each type of financial firm to be a source of systemic risk is evaluated in Douglas Elliot, "Regulating Systemically Important Financial Institutions That Are Not Banks," Brookings Institution, working paper, May 9, 2013, available at http://www.brookings.edu/research/papers/2013/05/09-regulating-financial-institutions-elliott.

[85] Whether all non-bank firms or only TBTF ones performing a given financial activity are important sources of systemic risk is beyond the scope of this report, but if all were, a case could be made that a prudential regulatory regime should be applied uniformly to all such firms, and not just large ones.

[86] See Office of Financial Research, *Asset Management and Financial Stability*, September 2013, http://www.treasury.gov/initiatives/ofr/research/Documents/OFR_AMFS_FINAL.pdf; Douglas Elliott, "Systemic Risk and the Asset Management Industry," Brookings Institution, May 2014.

[87] This is discussed in more detail in the Appendix. See also Arthur Wilmarth, "The Dodd-Frank Act: A Flawed and Inadequate Response to the Too-Big-To-Fail Problem," *Oregon Law Review*, vol. 89, April 6, 2011, p. 951.

[88] Dafna Avraham, et al., "Peeling the Onion: A Structural View of U.S. Bank Holding Companies," *Liberty Street Economics*, July 20, 2012, available at

http://libertystreeteconomics.newyorkfed.org/2012/07/peeling-the-onion-astructural-view-of-us-bank-holding-companies.html#.U-TnELFgi68.

[89] See, for example, Thomas Hoenig, "Back to Basics: A Better Alternative to Basel Capital Rules," Federal Deposit Insurance Corporation, speech delivered to the American Banker Regulatory Symposium, September 14, 2012.

[90] This issue was discussed by the Attorney General at a 2013 hearing. See U.S. Congress, Senate Judiciary Committee, *Oversight of the U.S. Department of Justice*, 113th Cong., 1st sess., March 6, 2013.

[91] During the debate of the Dodd-Frank Act, policy makers considered keeping the identities of regulated firms confidential, but they concluded that this would be impractical.

[92] Congressional Budget Office, *Measuring the Capital Positions of Fannie Mae and Freddie Mac*, June 2006.

[93] For an in-depth discussion, see the section in the Appendix entitled "Fannie Mae and Freddie Mac."

[94] Office of Federal Housing Enterprise Oversight, "Fannie Mae and Freddie Mac Capital," *Mortgage Market Note 08- 2*, July 17, 2008.

[95] Assuming that the overall supply of credit remained constant, raising the cost of capital at TBTF firms would reduce the amount of credit supplied to those firms, thereby increasing the supply of credit available to other firms. Economic theory predicts that the greater supply of credit available to other firms would reduce their cost of capital.

[96] FSOC issued a final rule in April 2012. It can be accessed at http://www.treasury.gov/initiatives/fsoc/rulemaking/Documents/Authority%20to%20Require%20Supervision%20and%20Regulation%20of%20Certain%20Nonbank%20Financial%20 Companies.pdf.

[97] GE Capital is often referred to as a non-bank lender because it does not mainly fund its loans through deposits. Nevertheless, it is chartered as a savings and loan holding company.

[98] Information on designated firms can be accessed at http://www.treasury.gov/initiatives/fsoc/designations/Pages/ default.aspx.

[99] The complaint can be accessed at http://online.wsj.com/public/resources/documents/011315metlife.pdf. For more information, see CRS Report WSLG1164, *MetLife's SIFI Designation Goes to Court*, by M. Maureen Murphy.

[100] GE, Conference Call (Transcript), April 10, 2015, http://www.ge.com/sites/default/files/ge_webcast_transcript_04102015_0.pdf.

[101] A current list of top 50 depositories by asset size is available at http://www.ffiec.gov/nicpubweb/nicweb/ Top50Form.aspx. Some of the firms on this list are not bank holding companies. Other types of depositories, such as savings and loan holding companies, with more than $50 billion in assets are not subject to the final rule, but the Fed has indicated that it intends to propose rulemaking in the future that apply to them.

[102] The rule, "Enhanced Prudential Standards for Bank Holding Companies and Foreign Banking Organizations," can be accessed at http://federalreserve.gov/newsevents/press/bcreg/20140218a.htm.

[103] The Congressional Research Service was not able to locate an official list of banks subject to Title I enhanced supervision. In 2015, 31 BHCs were subject to the Title I Federal Reserve stress tests because they had over $50 billion in assets. See Federal Reserve, *Dodd-Frank Act Stress Test 2015*, March 2015, http://www.federalreserve.gov/ newsevents/press/bcreg/bcreg20150305a1.pdf. About 130 banks (foreign and domestic) have submitted resolution plans ("living wills") pursuant to Title I, however. See Chairman Martin Gruenberg, testimony before the Senate Committee on Banking, Housing, and Urban Affairs, September 9, 2014, p. 5, available at http://www.banking.senate.gov/public/index.cfm?

FuseAction=Hearings.Testimony&Hearing_ID=b15fc832-df18-47d7-8c7d-1367e5770086 &Witness_ID=c15856a4-8f8c-4958-ad7c-a385bb31c3f8.

[104] FSB, "Policy Measures to Address Systemically Important Financial Institutions," November 4, 2011, http://www.financialstabilityboard.org/publications/r_111104bb.pdf. The identification methodology is described in Basel Committee on Banking Supervision, "Global Systemically Important Banks: Assessment Methodology," *Consultative Document*, July 2011, http://www.bis.org/publ/bcbs201.pdf.

[105] FSB, "2014 Update of Global Systemically Important Banks," November 6, 2014, http://www.financialstabilityboard.org/wp-content/uploads/r_141106b.pdf. The FSB is an international forum of which the United States is a member.

[106] The rule applies to all banks with more than $700 billion in assets, and was set at that level to include all banks designated as "global systemically important banks" G-SIBs. The rule can be viewed at http://federalreserve.gov/ newsevents/press/bcreg/20140408a.htm.

[107] Many provisions of the Basel III Accord were adopted in rulemaking in July 2013. The 2013 final rule does not include the capital surcharge for G-SIBs, which regulators have announced will be proposed at a later date. For more information, see http://federalreserve.gov/bankinforeg/basel/USImplementation.htm.

[108] Bank for International Settlements, *Basel III Summary Table*, http://www.bis.org/bcbs/basel3/b3summarytable.pdf.

[109] The rule, "Risk-Based Capital Guidelines: Implementation of Capital Requirements for Global Systemically Important Bank Holding Companies," can be accessed at http://www.federalreserve.gov/newsevents/press/bcreg/ 20141209a.htm.

[110] The final rule, "Liquidity Coverage Ratio: Liquidity Risk Measurement Standards," can be accessed at http://www.gpo.gov/fdsys/pkg/FR-2014-10-10/pdf/2014-22520.pdf.

[111] FSB, "2014 Update of List of Global Systemically Important Insurers," November 6, 2014, http://www.financialstabilityboard.org/wp-content/uploads/r_141106a.pdf.

[112] FSB, "Assessment Methodologies for Identifying Non-Bank Non-Insurer Global Systemically Important Financial Institutions," January 8, 2014, http://www.financialstabilityboard.org/publications/r_140108.htm.

[113] Hon. Jeb Hensarling et al, "Letter to Secretary Lew, Chair White, and Chair Yellen," May 9, 2014.

[114] Gary Stern and Ron Feldman, *Too Big to Fail* (Washington, DC: Brookings Institution Press), 2004.

[115] An alternative view is that Lehman Brothers' bankruptcy was more disruptive because the rescue of Bear Stearns led creditors to conclude that other large investment banks would also be rescued.

[116] The Fed has issued a proposed rule to implement these standards, which can be accessed at http://www.federalreserve.gov/newsevents/press/bcreg/bcreg20111220a1.pdf.

[117] For more information, see CRS Report R41398, *The Dodd-Frank Wall Street Reform and Consumer Protection Act: Title VII, Derivatives*, by Rena S. Miller and Kathleen Ann Ruane.

[118] For more information, see CRS Report R41529, *Supervision of U.S. Payment, Clearing, and Settlement Systems: Designation of Financial Market Utilities (FMUs)*, by Marc Labonte.

[119] For more information, see CRS Report R40530, *Insolvency of Systemically Significant Financial Companies (SSFCs): Bankruptcy vs. Conservatorship/Receivership*, by David H. Carpenter.

[120] See CRS Report RL34657, *Financial Institution Insolvency: Federal Authority over Fannie Mae, Freddie Mac, and Depository Institutions*, by David H. Carpenter and M. Maureen Murphy.

[121] For more information on purchase and assumption and other resolution methods, see the section below entitled "Resolution of Banks Before and After the Federal Deposit Insurance Corporation Improvement Act."

[122] For more information, see the section below entitled "Fannie Mae and Freddie Mac."

[123] See, for example, Sheila Bair, "We Must Resolve to End Too Big to Fail," remarks at the 47th Annual Conference on Bank Structure and Competition, Federal Reserve Bank of Chicago, May 5, 2011, http://www.fdic.gov/bank/analytical/quarterly/2011_vol5_2/Article1.pdf.

[124] For more information, see CRS Report RS22950, *Fannie Mae and Freddie Mac in Conservatorship*, by Mark Jickling.

[125] For more information, see "Washington Mutual and Wachovia." The Fortune list can be accessed at http://money.cnn.com/magazines/fortune/fortune500/2007/full_list/index.html.

[126] The FDIC gives a detailed explanation of how the failure of a firm like Lehman Brothers could have been managed more smoothly under a resolution regime in "The Orderly Liquidation of Lehman Brothers Holdings Under the Dodd-Frank Act," *FDIC Quarterly*, vol. 5, no. 2, 2011, p. 31, http://www.fdic.gov/bank/analytical/quarterly/2011_vol5_2/lehman.pdf.

[127] See, for example, Jeffrey Lacker and John Weinberg, "Now How Large is the Safety Net?" *Economic Brief 10-06*, June 2010, http://www.richmondfed.org/publications/research/economic_brief/2010/pdf/eb_10-06.pdf.

[128] See, for example, Kenneth Scott and John Taylor, "How to Let Too Big to Fail Banks Fail," *Wall Street Journal*, May 16, 2013, p. A15; Hoover Institute, Resolution Project publications, available at http://www.hoover.org/ taskforces/economic-policy/resolution-project/publications. For a comparison, see Sabrina Pellerin and John Walter, "Orderly Liquidation Authority as an Alternative to Bankruptcy," Federal Reserve Bank of Richmond, *Economic Quarterly*, vol. 98, no. 1, First Quarter 2012, p. 1.

[129] International Monetary Fund, "Resolution of Cross-Border Banks – A Proposed Framework for Enhanced Coordination," June 2010, available at http://www.imf.org/external/np/pp/eng/2010/061110.pdf.

[130] For more information, see CRS Report RL34623, *Housing and Economic Recovery Act of 2008*, coordinated by N. Eric Weiss.

[131] For more information, see CRS Report RL34657, *Financial Institution Insolvency: Federal Authority over Fannie Mae, Freddie Mac, and Depository Institutions*, by David H. Carpenter and M. Maureen Murphy. Before HERA, Fannie Mae's and Freddie Mac's regulator had more limited powers of conservatorship and no powers of receivership.

[132] Martin J. Gruenberg, Acting Chairman of the Federal Deposit Insurance Corporation, Remarks to the Federal Reserve Bank of Chicago Bank Structure Conference; Chicago, IL, May 10, 2012.

[133] It can be accessed here: http://www.gpo.gov/fdsys/pkg/FR-2013-12-18/pdf/2013-30057.pdf. For more information on the FDIC as receiver under Title II, see http://www.fdic.gov/resauthority/.

[134] Christopher Payne and Tony Costello, "Will Orderly Resolution Work?," *BGOV Analysis*, May 19, 2014.

[135] Gov. Daniel Tarullo, "Dodd-Frank Implementation," Testimony before the Senate Banking Committee, September 9, 2014, http://www.federalreserve.gov/newsevents/testimony/tarullo20140909a.htm.

[136] 70 Stat. 133.

[137] For more information on the erosion of Glass Steagall, see CRS Report R41181, *Permissible Securities Activities of Commercial Banks Under the Glass-Steagall Act (GSA) and the Gramm-Leach-Bliley Act (GLBA)*, by David H. Carpenter and M. Maureen Murphy.

[138] For more information, see Mark Greenlee, "Historical Review of 'Umbrella Regulation' by the Board of Governors of the Federal Reserve System," Federal Reserve Bank of Cleveland, working paper 08-07, October 2008.

[139] For more information, see CRS Report 94-744, *The Riegle-Neal Interstate Banking and Branching Efficiency Act of 1994*, by M. Maureen Murphy. (This report is out of print, but available by request.)

[140] See General Accounting Office, *Guidelines for Rescuing Large Failing Firms and Municipalities*, GAO Report GGD-84-34, March 29, 1984; CRS Report R41401, *General Motors' Initial Public Offering: Review of Issues and Implications for TARP*, by Bill Canis, Baird Webel, and Gary Shorter; CRS Report R41940, *TARP Assistance for Chrysler: Restructuring and Repayment Issues*, by Baird Webel and Bill Canis.

[141] For more information on the resolution process, see CRS Report RL34657, *Financial Institution Insolvency: Federal Authority over Fannie Mae, Freddie Mac, and Depository Institutions*, by David H. Carpenter and M. Maureen Murphy.

[142] Federal Deposit Insurance Corporation, *Managing The Crisis*, Part 1, Chapter 3, August 1998, http://www.fdic.gov/ bank/historical/managing/history1-03.pdf.

[143] Gary Stern and Ron Feldman, *Too Big to Fail*, (Washington, D.C.: Brookings Institution Press), 2004, p. 151.

[144] Federal Deposit Insurance Corporation, *Managing The Crisis*, Part 1, Chapter 5, August 1998, p. 153, http://www.fdic.gov/bank/historical/managing/history1-05.pdf.

[145] Federal Deposit Insurance Corporation, "Continental Illinois and 'Too Big to Fail'," *History of the Eighties*, Ch. 7, http://www.fdic.gov/bank/historical/history/235_258.pdf.

[146] Besides FDIC resolutions, there were a large number of thrift resolutions in the 1980s. Since these institutions tended to be small, this experience is not central to the TBTF issue.

[147] FDIC, "The Savings and Loan Crisis and Its Relationship to Banking," *History of the Eighties – Lessons for the Future*, December 1997, Ch. 4, http://www.fdic.gov/bank/ historical/history/.

[148] The Federal Deposit Insurance Corporation Improvement Act, P.L. 102-242. Previously, the FDIC had to demonstrate that its resolution method was less costly than an insured deposit payoff; that requirement could be waived in the case of the "essentiality" exception noted above.

[149] FDIC data on bank failures can be accessed at http://www2.fdic.gov/hsob/SelectRpt.asp? EntryTyp=30.

[150] 12 U.S.C 1823(c).

[151] Federal Reserve annual report quoted in Anna Schwartz, "The Misuse of the Fed's Discount Window," *Federal Reserve Bank of St. Louis Review*, September/October 1992, p. 58.

[152] For more information on the Fed's response to the Penn Central failure, see Mark Carlson and David Wheelock, "The Lender of Last Resort: Lessons from the Fed's First 100 Years," Federal Reserve Bank of St. Louis, working paper 2012-056B, February 2013.

[153] Mark Carlson and David Wheelock, "The Lender of Last Resort: Lessons from the Fed's First 100 Years," Federal Reserve Bank of St. Louis, Working Paper 2012-056B, February 2013.

[154] Federal Deposit Insurance Corporation, "Continental Illinois National Bank and Trust Company," *Managing The Crisis*, Part 2, Chapter 4, August 1998, http://www.fdic.gov/ bank/historical/managing/history2-04.pdf.

[155] Federal Deposit Insurance Corporation, "Continental Illinois and 'Too Big to Fail'," *History of the Eighties*, ch. 7, http://www.fdic.gov/bank/historical/history/235_258.pdf.

[156] The claim that more than 100 banks would have failed has been disputed in Larry Wall, "Too Big to Fail After FDICIA," *Federal Reserve Bank of Atlanta Economic Review*, no. 78, January/February 1993, p. 1.

[157] Federal Deposit Insurance Corporation, "Continental Illinois National Bank and Trust Company," *Managing The Crisis*, Part 2, Chapter 4, August 1998, http://www.fdic.gov/bank/historical/managing/history2-04.pdf.

[158] The role of regulatory supervision in Continental Illinois' failure is discussed in Federal Deposit Insurance Corporation, "Continental Illinois and 'Too Big to Fail'," *History of the Eighties*, Ch. 7, http://www.fdic.gov/bank/ historical/history/235_258.pdf.

[159] Office of the Comptroller of the Currency, "Statement on Continental Illinois," news release 84-45, May 10, 1984.

[160] Tim Carrington, "U.S. Won't Let 11 Biggest Banks in Nation Fail," *Wall Street Journal*, September 20, 1984, p. 1.

[161] Donald Morgan and Kevin Stiroh, *Too Big to Fail After All These Years*, Federal Reserve Bank of New York, Staff Report Number 220, New York, NY, September 2005.

[162] For more details, see U.S. General Accounting Office, *Long-Term Capital Management*, GGD-00-3, October 1999, http://www.gao.gov/archive/2000/gg00003.pdf.

[163] Kevin Dowd, *Too Big to Fail? Long-Term Capital Management and the Federal Reserve*, Cato Institute, Briefing Paper Number 52, Washington, DC, September 1999, http://www.cato.org/pubs/briefs/bp52.pdf.

[164] The increase in leverage was more pronounced at investment banks than commercial banks. See, for example Sebnem Kalemli-Ozcan, Bent Sorensen, Sevcan Yesiltas, "Leverage Across Firms, Banks, and Countries," working paper, August 2011.

[165] For more detailed information, see CRS Report RL34427, *Financial Turmoil: Federal Reserve Policy Responses*, by Marc Labonte.

[166] Bear Stearns complied with an SEC net capital rule, but was not subject to safety and soundness supervision. For more information, see CRS Report R43087, *Who Regulates Whom and How? An Overview of U.S. Financial Regulatory Policy for Banking and Securities Markets*, by Edward V. Murphy.

[167] Securities and Exchange Commission, "Statement of SEC Division of Trading and Markets Regarding The Bear Stearns Companies," press release 2008-44, March 11, 2008, http://www.sec.gov/news/press/2008/2008-44.htm.

[168] List can be accessed at http://money.cnn.com/magazines/fortune/fortune500/2007/full_list/index.html.

[169] Greg Ip, "Central Bank Offers Loans to Brokers, Cuts Key Rate," *Wall Street Journal*, March 17, 2008, p. A1.

[170] Federal Reserve Bank of New York, "New York Fed Completes Financing Arrangement Related to JPMorgan Chase's Acquisition of Bear Stearns," press release, June 26, 2008.

[171] Federal Reserve Bank of New York, "Statement on Financing Arrangement of JPMorgan Chase's Acquisition of Bear Stearns," press release, March 24, 2008.

[172] Congressional Budget Office, *The Budgetary Impact and Subsidy Costs of the Federal Reserve's Actions During the Financial Crisis*, May 2010.

[173] Lending records can be accessed at http://www.federalreserve.gov/newsevents/reform_pdcf.htm.

[174] Securities and Exchange Commission, "Statement of SEC Division of Trading and Markets Regarding The Bear Stearns Companies," press release 2008-44, March 11, 2008, http://www.sec.gov/news/press/2008/2008-44.htm.

[175] J.P. Morgan Chase, Annual Report, 2008, p. 9, http://files.shareholder.com/downloads/ONE/2506919982x0x283416/66cc70ba-5410-43c4-b20b-181974bc6be6/2008_AR_Complete_AR.pdf.

[176] Short selling consists of borrowing shares and selling them, in the hope that the short seller can buy back the borrowed shares at a lower price in the future. A short sale is "naked" if the seller does not actually borrow shares for delivery to the buyer. For more information, see CRS Report RS22099, *Regulation of Naked Short Selling*, by Mark Jickling.

[177] Kara Scannell and Tom Lauricella, "SEC Extends Short-Selling Rules," *Wall Street Journal*, July 30, 2008, p. C. 1.

[178] Limits on OFHEO's powers and independence are discussed in CRS Report RL32069, *Improving the Effectiveness of GSE Oversight: Legislative Proposals in the 108th Congress*, by Loretta Nott and Mark Jickling.

[179] Office of Federal Housing Enterprise Oversight, Statement of OFHEO Director James B. Lockhart, July 10, 2008.

[180] For more information, see CRS Report RL34661, *Fannie Mae's and Freddie Mac's Financial Problems*, by N. Eric Weiss.

[181] For more information, see Federal Housing Finance Agency, U.S. Treasury Support for Fannie Mae and Freddie Mac," Mortgage Market Note, no. 10-1, Jan. 20, 2010.

[182] U.S. Treasury, "Treasury Department Announces Further Steps to Expedite Wind Down of Fannie Mae and Freddie Mac," press release, August 16, 2012. The agreement allows the GSEs to build a capital reserve of $3 billion.

[183] Congressional Budget Office, *The Budgetary Cost of Fannie Mae and Freddie Mac*, Testimony before the Committee on the Budget, U.S. House of Representatives, June 2011.

[184] List can be accessed at http://money.cnn.com/magazines/fortune/fortune500/2007/full_list/index.html.

[185] For more information, see CRS Report R43087, *Who Regulates Whom and How? An Overview of U.S. Financial Regulatory Policy for Banking and Securities Markets*, by Edward V. Murphy.

[186] http://www.bankruptcydata.com/Research/Largest_Overall_All-Time.pdf.

[187] For example, see Chairman Ben Bernanke, "Lessons from the Failure of Lehman Brothers," testimony before the Committee on Financial Services, U.S. House of Representatives, April 20, 2010, http://www.federalreserve.gov/ newsevents/testimony/bernanke20100420a.htm. Thomas Baxter, testimony before the Financial Crisis Inquiry Commission, September 1, 2010, http://fcic-static.law.stanford.edu/cdn_media/fcic-testimony/2010-0901-Baxter.pdf.

[188] See CRS Report R40928, *Lehman Brothers and IndyMac: Comparing Resolution Regimes*, by David H. Carpenter.

[189] Michael Fleming and Asani Sarkar, "The Failure Resolution of Lehman Brothers," Federal Reserve Bank of New York, *Economic Policy Review*, vol. 20, no. 2, March 2014.

[190] Figure cited in Fed Chairman Ben Bernanke, "Financial Reform to Address Systemic Risk," speech at the Council on Foreign Relations, March 10, 2009, http://www.federalreserve.gov/newsevents/speech/bernanke20090310a.htm.

[191] There is debate over whether the money market run triggered by Lehman Brothers' bankruptcy should be considered to be caused by Lehman Brothers being TBTF. The view that attributes the run to TBTF interprets the run as triggered by concerns about the exposure of Lehman Brothers counterparties. The alternative view is that the run was

triggered by concerns about holding paper issued by any financial firm with exposure to "toxic" MBS. Neither view is inconsistent with the fact that many of the funds that experienced runs were not holding paper issued by Lehman Brothers. See, for example, Daniel Tarullo, "Regulating Systemic Risk," speech at 2011 Credit Markets Symposium, Charlotte, North Carolina, March 31, 2011, http://www.federalreserve.gov/newsevents/speech/ tarullo20110331a.htm.

[192] This section draws on information from CRS Report R41073, *Government Interventions in Response to Financial Turmoil*, by Baird Webel and Marc Labonte.

[193] Thomas Baxter, testimony before the Financial Crisis Inquiry Commission, September 1, 2010, http://fcicstatic.law.stanford.edu/cdn_media/fcic-testimony/2010-0901-Baxter.pdf.

[194] Data from http://www.federalreserve.gov/newsevents/reform_pdcf.htm.

[195] See CRS Report R40438, *Federal Government Assistance for American International Group (AIG)*, by Baird Webel.

[196] Craig Torres and Hugh Son, "Bernanke Says Insurer AIG Operated Like a Hedge Fund," *Bloomberg*, March 3, 2009.

[197] Scott Polakoff, Testimony before the Subcommittee on Capital Markets, Insurance, and Government Sponsored Enterprises, House Committee on Financial Services, U.S. House of Representatives, March 18, 2009, http://www.house.gov/apps/list/hearing/financialsvcs_dem/ots_3.18.09.pdf.

[198] List can be accessed at http://money.cnn.com/magazines/fortune/fortune 500/2007/full_list/index.html.

[199] Chairman Ben Bernanke, Testimony Before the House Committee on Financial Services, March 24, 2009.

[200] Congressional Budget Office, *Report on the Troubled Asset Relief Program*, April 2014, Table 3. The day after the failure of WaMu, Wachovia Bank depositors accelerated the withdrawal of significant amounts from their accounts. In addition, wholesale funds providers withdrew liquidity support from Wachovia. It appeared likely that Wachovia would soon become unable to fund its operations.[204]

[201] List can be accessed at http://money.cnn.com/magazines/fortune/fortune500/2007/full_list/index.html. Scott G. Alvarez, "The Acquisition of Wachovia Corporation by Wells Fargo & Company," Testimony Before the Financial Crisis Inquiry Commission, Washington, D.C., September 1, 2010.

[202] Kirsten Grind, "WaMu's Final Days," *Puget Sound Business Journal*, Friday, September 25, 2009, http://seattle.bizjournals.com/seattle/stories/2009/09/28/story1.html?page=1.

[203] Federal Deposit Insurance Corporation, "JPMorgan Chase Acquires Banking Operations of Washington Mutual," Press Release PR-85-2008, September 25, 2008.

[204] Scott G. Alvarez, "The Acquisition of Wachovia Corporation by Wells Fargo & Company," Testimony Before the Financial Crisis Inquiry Commission, Washington, D.C., September 1, 2010, http://www.federalreserve.gov/ newsevents/testimony/alvarez20100901a.htm.

[205] *Ibid.*

[206] *Ibid.*

[207] Federal Reserve, "Statement by the Board of Governors of the Federal Reserve System Regarding the Application and Notices by Wells Fargo and Company to Acquire Wachovia Corporation," October 12, 2008, p. 7, http://www.federalreserve.gov/newsevents/press/orders/orders20081021a1.pdf.

[208] For more information on all TARP programs, see CRS Report R41427, *Troubled Asset Relief Program (TARP): Implementation and Status*, by Baird Webel.

[209] U.S. Department of Treasury, *TARP Monthly 105(a) Report – December 2011*, January 2012. The largest failure was CIT Group, with $76 billion in consolidated assets in the first quarter of 2009.

[210] Congressional Budget Office, *Report on the Troubled Asset Relief Program*, October 2012.

[211] In their regulatory call reports, banks report capital ratios for three measures: Total Risk-Based Capital, Tier 1 Risk-Based Capital, and Tier 1 Leverage. For large BHCs, the Fed sets a minimum Tier 1 leverage requirement of 3% of total assets for banks receiving the highest regulatory rating and 4% of total assets for all other firms (12 CFR 225 Appendix D). The regulatory rating that firms receive is confidential. For Tier 1 Risk-Based Capital and Total Risk-Based Capital, respectively, the Fed sets minimum requirements of 4% and 8% of risk-weighted assets.

[212] At the holding company level, Citigroup reported $118.8 billion of Tier 1 Capital in its December 2008 call report; of this total, $45 billion was from TARP. An estimate for the other two regulatory capital ratio measures cannot be easily calculated.

[213] 12 CFR Part 225, Subpart J.

[214] Citigroup, "Citi to Exchange Preferred Securities for Common, Increasing Tangible Common Equity to as Much as $81 Billion," press release, February 27, 2009, http://www.citigroup.com/citi/press/2009/090227a.htm.

[215] List can be accessed at http://money.cnn.com/magazines/fortune/fortune500/2007/full_list/index.html.

[216] Henry Paulson, Testimony before the Committee on Oversight and Government Reform, U.S. House of Representatives, July 16, 2009, posted at http://online.wsj.com/public/resources/documents/WSJ-20090715- PaulsonTestimony.pdf.

[217] The first quarter of 2009 was the first call report to incorporate TARP shares and the Merrill Lynch merger. In their regulatory call reports, banks report capital ratios for three measures: Total Risk-Based Capital, Tier 1 Risk-Based Capital, and Tier 1 Leverage. For large BHCs, the Fed sets a minimum Tier 1 leverage requirement of 3% of total assets for banks receiving the highest regulatory rating and 4% of total assets for all other firms (12 CFR 225 Appendix D). The regulatory rating that firms receive is confidential. For Tier 1 Risk-Based Capital and Total Risk-Based Capital, respectively, the Fed sets minimum requirements of 4% and 8% of risk-weighted assets.

[218] At the holding company level, Bank of America reported $117.9 billion of Tier 1 Capital in its December 2008 call report; of this total, $45 billion was from TARP. An estimate for the other two capital ratio measures cannot easily be calculated.

[219] Federal Reserve, *The Supervisory Capital Assessment Program: Overview of Results*, May 7, 2009. For an evaluation, see Special Inspector General for Troubled Asset Relief Program, *Exiting TARP: Repayments by the Largest Financial Institutions*, SIGTARP report 11-005, September 29, 2011.

[220] Citigroup, *Supervisory Capital Assessment Program Results – Update on Exchange Offer*, May 7, 2009, http://www.citigroup.com/citi/fin/data/p090507a.pdf.

[221] U.S. Treasury, "Treasury Prices Sale of Citigroup Subordinated Notes for Proceeds of $894 Million," press release, February 5, 2013.

[222] Congressional Budget Office, *Report on the Troubled Asset Relief Program*, April 2014.

[223] More information can be found in out-of-print CRS Report R40003, *U.S. Motor Vehicle Industry: Federal Financial Assistance and Restructuring*, coordinated by Bill Canis, available upon request.

[224] Congressional Oversight Panel, *January Oversight Report*, January 13, 2011, p. 82.

[225] CRS Report R41846, *Government Assistance for GMAC/Ally Financial: Unwinding the Government Stake*, by Baird Webel and Bill Canis.

[226] Congressional Budget Office, *Report on the Troubled Asset Relief Program*, April 2014, p. 6.

INDEX

C

D

E

F

G

H

I

J

L

M

N

O

P

R

S

T

U

V

W